Foundations of Medieval History
General Editor M.T. Clanchy

FOUNDATIONS OF MEDIEVAL HISTORY

Already published:

The Medieval Inquisition

Bernard Hamilton

Holmes & Meier Publishers, Inc
New York

Published in the United States of America by
Holmes & Meier Publishers, Inc.
30 Irving Place, New York, N.Y. 10003

Library of Congress Cataloging in Publication Data

Hamilton, Bernard, 1932–
  The medieval inquisition.

  (Foundations of medieval history)
  Bibliography: p. 100
  Includes index.
  1. Inquisition.   I. Title.   II. Series.
BX1712.H26   1981   272'.2   80-27997

ISBN 0-8419-0695-5

Manufactured in the United States of America

Contents

General preface

The purpose of this series is to provide concise and authoritative introductions to fundamental developments in medieval history. The books are designed to enable students both to master the basic facts about a topic and to form their own point of view. The authors, on their side, have an opportunity to write at greater length — and with more freedom — than in a chapter of a general textbook and, at the same time, to reach out to a wider audience than a specialist monograph commands.

In the present book Dr Hamilton, an expert on medieval religious history in both eastern and western Europe, discusses the controversial subject of heresy and its prosecution by the Inquisition. The subject is fraught with problems. How is heresy to be defined? Was it different from religious doubt or anti-clericalism? Why did heresy increase and what rules governed the inquisitors, making them different from other enforcers of orthodoxy? As well as answering these technical questions in a clear and factual way, Dr Hamilton faces up to the value judgements involved in assessing an institution which has a sinister reputation to this day. He shows that the inquisitors intended to convert heretics through spiritual penances rather than to burn and torture them indiscriminately as lay society often demanded. On the other hand, the pastoral purpose of the Inquisition could itself lead to injustice because inquisitors were not usually trained as lawyers but as spiritual directors. This study raises questions about the interaction of religion and law, and divine and human justice, which extend beyond Europe and the Middle Ages. An institution with a high moral purpose was turned to secular ends. Thus Philip IV of France used the Inquisition to destroy the Knights Templar, the élite of crusading chivalry. As Dr Hamilton points out, persecution and cruelty were not a monopoly of the Middle Ages and still less of the Inquisition. Nevertheless the institution of the Inquisition at the time when the papacy was at the height of its power in the first half of the thirteenth century must bear some of the burden of man's inhumanity to man in the centuries which followed. The medieval Inquisition led indirectly at the Reformation to the novel Spanish Inquisition, to the persecution of witches in Protestant countries, and it was even used by Calvin. These developments fall at the limit of Dr Hamilton's period, as his subject is the original medieval Inquisition. He takes his main story from the growth of Catharism in the twelfth century up to the trials of Joan of Arc and Gilles de Rais in the fifteenth.

M. T. Clanchy

THE LANDS OF THE MEDIEVAL INQUISITION

Introduction

Most people associate the word 'Inquisition' either with the Spanish Inquisition or with the Roman Inquisition which tried Galileo. Both these institutions were creations of the early modern period, but they had evolved from the medieval Inquisition, founded by Pope Gregory IX in the thirteenth century. That was, in some ways, a very different organization from the Inquisitions of the sixteenth century. In the Middle Ages much of Europe was divided into provinces, each of which was administered by an inquisitor who had a personal commission from the pope to examine cases of heresy in his area. There was no central department to direct and co-ordinate this work, and individual inquisitors had no institutional connection with their colleagues in other provinces, though they all exercised identical powers which were defined in canon law. This strange situation has led Kieckhofer in his *Repression of Heresy in Medieval Germany* to question whether it is useful to speak of a medieval Inquisition at all, rather than of papal commissions to make inquisition for heresy. This is not a view which I share, otherwise I should not have written this book.

The first comprehensive history of the Inquisition in the Middle Ages to be written in modern times was the work of H.C.Lea, which was published in three volumes in 1888. It has stood the test of time remarkably well, and Lea's chapters on the organization and procedures of the Inquisition were re-published, with an historical introduction by W.Ullmann, in 1963. Of course, a great deal of work has been done in the past 92 years on medieval heresy, and this has made some of Lea's historical chapters obsolete. But no definitive new history of the subject has yet appeared, and anybody working in this field will know how necessary it still is to have recourse to Lea's work on some points.

I should like to make it clear that this book is not intended to be a new, definitive account of the medieval Inquisition: it would be impossible to achieve that in a work of this length. This study is a work of synthesis, not of original research, and is intended for the use of people who want an introduction to the subject, and who may not be very familiar with the historical context in which the Inquisition operated.

I have attempted, as far as possible, to look at the Inquisition in action, rather than as it existed in the minds of the canon lawyers who defined its powers. There are excellent studies of the juridical status of the Inquisition, which are listed in the bibliography, and it would be pointless to try to duplicate those works. There is, however, a vast difference between the powers which any institution may possess in theory and the extent to which it can use them in practice. A story used to circulate in Rome in the reign of Pius XII of how the pope had once said to a cardinal who was urging him to solve some ecclesiastical dispute by papal fiat: 'you forget, your eminence, that I do not have the powers of an Irish bishop'. Some inquisitors would, I think, have sympathized with Pope Pius: on paper their powers were almost unlimited; in practice they might find it difficult to secure the arrest of a notorious heretic who lived in the same town as themselves.

The history of the Inquisition is in some ways very depressing. Cruelty and intolerance are common to most societies in most ages, but the Inquisition is unusual in that many of the men who administered it were very gifted, sometimes even spiritually gifted, and were justly considered eminent by their contemporaries and in some cases worthy of canonization after their death. Yet these men shared the belief of their society that it was morally wrong to tolerate error, and meritorious to use physical coercion against religious dissenters. Despite this, the history of the Inquisition is a source of hope, since it shows that it is impossible to coerce belief. The inquisitors could, within limits, enforce outward conformity, but they never succeeded in producing by those methods a united Christendom whose members all shared a single faith, which was their object. The history of their failure forms a valuable part of western European experience.

Acknowledgements

I should like to express my thanks to the librarians of the following institutions which I have used while working on this book, and to their staffs: the British Library, the University of Nottingham Library, the University of London Library, the Warburg Institute, Dr Williams's Library and the London Library.

I should also like to thank Dr M.C.Barber of the University of Reading for his advice about the rôle of the Inquisition in the trial of the Templars. If I have made any errors of fact or interpretation in that section of the book the responsibility is, of course, entirely my own. I am particularly grateful to my medieval colleagues in the Department of History at the University of Nottingham, who, at some cost to themselves, have arranged their teaching and my own in order to give me time to write this book. Finally, and chiefly, my thanks go to my family: to my wife who has made valuable (though unacknowledged) contributions to this work by some of the suggestions she has made when I have discussed it with her; and to my children, who have sustained me while I wrote with unsolicited cups of coffee.

Bernard Hamilton
Nottingham
1 June 1980

1
Heresy and the medieval Church

The Inquisition evolved as a means of prosecuting heresy through a system of special ecclesiastical tribunals. The Greek word *hairesis* meant choice and initially had a neutral connotation. But in the early Christian centuries the term was applied to the choice of doctrines different from those of the Great Church, and it subsequently retained this pejorative meaning of erroneous choice. Heresy might consist either in rejecting a doctrine which the Church taught, or in teaching a new doctrine which the Church had not sanctioned. Orthodox theologians always regarded heresy as a sin which debarred those who professed it from the sacraments, but in Western Europe in the central Middle Ages it was also considered a crime, punishable by law, and the Inquisition was brought into being to deal with it.

Our own society has tolerated the public expression of a diversity of opinions about religious matters for almost 200 years and as a result of this medieval attitudes towards religious conformity are very alien to us. Since the Inquisition can only be understood in the context of the society of which it formed part, it is necessary to begin by examining the place of the Church in that society, for without an accepted orthodoxy there could have been no heresy and had there been no heresy the Inquisition would not have been set up.

It is a commonplace that in the Middle Ages there was only one Church in western Europe, the Catholic Church, instead of the diversity of confessions which have co-existed there since the Protestant reformation. The medieval Catholic Church has evolved, with no break in historical continuity, into the Catholic Church as it exists today, and its spiritual function has not changed in that period: to mediate the saving grace of Christ to the world through its sacraments and its teachings. Yet the social function of the Church has changed a great deal in the past thousand years, and this is not always sufficiently recognized by people unfamiliar with the Middle Ages.

People quite commonly think of medieval Catholicism in terms of modern societies, like those of Ireland or Poland, where the Catholic Church is strong. Such analogies are misleading, for

13

Catholicism in those countries has been profoundly shaped by the Counter-Reformation, which strove, with some success, to produce a well-instructed laity, with a high standard of regular religious practice and a deferential attitude towards the hierarchy. Medieval Catholicism was not like that at all, and a closer, though by no means exact, parallel might be found in modern Latin America, which has been Catholic for centuries, but is not noted for its religious fervour.

In the central Middle Ages Catholicism was the established religion of the British Isles, France, those parts of northern Spain reconquered from the Moors, Italy, Germany, Hungary, Bohemia, Poland, Scandinavia and Iceland. Virtually everybody in those areas was a member of the Church, the only exceptions being communities of Jews, and some Muslims in parts of Spain and Sicily recently regained from the Saracens. It is often assumed that because almost all people in the medieval west professed the Catholic religion, they were all moderately committed to the faith and practice of the Church. Nothing could be further from the truth.

In the first place many lay people were poorly instructed in the rudiments of their faith. This resulted from the fact that many of the lower clergy were badly educated: arrangements for training priests were made by individual bishops, and in some dioceses such facilities were minimal. An ill-instructed priest clearly could not catechize his parishioners adequately and even a well-educated one had few opportunities for doing so. The habit of regularly preaching at Mass on Sundays and holy days was a doubtful blessing which still lay in the future. Before the foundation of the mendicant orders in the thirteenth century many people only heard a sermon if the bishop visited their parish, and it was therefore possible in some rural areas to go through life without ever receiving any formal religious instruction at all.

Religious doubt

If ignorance of the faith was widespread, religious doubt was also common. Take, for example, this fragment of conversation among some southern French peasants who were chatting to each other in the main square of a village called Rabat in the early years of the fourteenth century. One of them, Bernard d'Orte, reported how:

> After we had been jesting for a little while I said to William's wife, Gentile, showing her my thumbs: 'Shall we come to life

again with this flesh and these bones? What an idea! I don't
believe it.'
(E. Le Roy Ladurie, *Montaillou. Cathars and Catholics in a
French village, 1294–1324,* translated by Barbara Bray,
London, 1978, p. 320.)

Such opinions were by no means uncommon in the central Middle
Ages. Then, as now, people entertained considerable doubts about
some of the central tenets of the Christian religion. Those most
commonly called in question were the Virgin birth, the resurrec-
tion of the body, and the doctrine of transubstantiation, all of
which are seemingly contrary to general human experience.
Religious doubt in the Middle Ages seems, indeed, to have been as
widespread and very similar in character to that which opinion
polls reveal as present in our own society.

Doubt is not to be confused with heresy. Heresy involves a
positive rejection of, or innovation in, some part or the whole of the
Church's received teaching, whereas doubt is negative and arises
from a lack of conviction about the truth of some orthodox
doctrine. The Church looked upon doubt as an endemic weakness,
inherent in man's fallen condition: even the Apostles had not been
immune from it, and Pope Gregory VII thought that nearly everybody experienced fundamental doubts about the truths of the
Christian faith at some time in their lives. Religious doubt was
never treated as a crime in the Middle Ages: it was regarded as a
temptation, and if wilfully persisted in could become a sin, but the
Church regarded spiritual counselling as the appropriate method
of dealing with it. Nevertheless, doubt and ignorance were sufficiently common in medieval society for the attacks which heretics
made on orthodox belief to have caused no general outrage. Many
people probably had misgivings about the truths of some of the
doctrines denounced by heretics, and their hostility towards
heresy stemmed from other causes than those of dogmatic dis-
agreement.

The generality of medieval Catholics do not seem to have been
particularly fervent in their religious practice either. Church
synods throughout the period found it necessary to re-enact the
same legislation about the abysmally low standards of Mass
attendance and reception of the sacraments by the laity; and it is
noteworthy that when, in the reign of King John, England was
placed under an interdict and the churches remained closed for five
years, hardly a single voice was raised in public protest. A parallel
degree of indifference to the availability of public worship would
be unthinkable in a post-Tridentine Catholic country. There were,
of course, social pressures at work in medieval society to enforce

certain minimal standards of religious conformity. There was general disapproval of women who conceived children in Lent and of knights who took up arms on Good Friday; but there is no evidence that such pressures extended to the enforcement of even casual church attendance or occasional communion. A corollary of this low standard of practice was, of course, that the clergy were held in no very high regard. The virulence of the attacks made throughout the Middle Ages on the Church hierarchy, from the pope and curia downwards, would have made the average Victorian free-thinker blench.

It would, of course, be a travesty to suggest that all lay people were wavering in their faith, negligent in their practice and rabidly anti-clerical. There were devout lay men and women who were orthodox in belief, punctilious in their religious duties and deferential towards their priests, but they seem to have been more uncommon in what are sometimes called 'the ages of faith' than they are today. If heretics aroused popular hostility it was not primarily because they reviled the clergy or absented themselves from church, since the majority of their orthodox neighbours seem to have behaved in much the same way.

The strength of the Church

The medieval Church was strong not because the majority of its lay members were, in the modern sense, fervent Catholics, but because it pervaded society at all levels in a way which has no parallel anywhere in the western world today. The most obvious example of this is that church and state in the Middle Ages were virtually co-terminous, for they were different aspects of a single society. The chief distinction between them was that whereas there were many states there was only one Church. At its head was the pope; and western Europe was divided, for ecclesiastical purposes, into provinces, each under a metropolitan archbishop, while each province was subdivided into a number of dioceses and each diocese into a number of parishes. The hierarchy was thus represented in every community by a parish priest and the Church controlled through the pulpit the only means of mass communication available in that age. All members of the western Church were subject to a single code of canon law, promulgated by the holy see, and this affected everybody because it regulated marriages and testamentary law and the whole range of penitential discipline. With minor regional variations a common liturgy was in use throughout western Europe, which was celebrated in Latin, and this was a unifying force because it was the one activity in which

all members of society, irrespective of race, class or sex, might
share.

The Church occupied a central place in the government,
administration and economic life of western Europe. In the
centuries that followed the break-up of the Roman Empire the
Church, as the sole vehicle of a more civilized tradition in a
barbarous world, became involved in social and political activities
which formed no part of its essential mission, but which it alone
was qualified to discharge. Because the clergy were the only
literate class in the early-medieval west they inevitably became
involved in the work of secular administration. One consequence
of this was that many prelates were given extensive powers of
secular jurisdiction. The Church became the greatest single land-
owner in western Europe: bishops and abbots in many cases had
authority over the peasants who worked their estates; and, in
parts of Europe where a feudal order obtained, they were responsible for supplying large numbers of knights to the royal armies.
Since the Church enjoyed so much power in the public life of
western Europe many of the most talented men of the age received
holy orders. We are still familiar with the concept of the scholar-
priest, and in the Middle Ages many of the most academically
gifted men were clergy, but a career in the Church then attracted
also a high proportion of the men who in our own society would be
in the top echelons of industrial management, the judiciary, the
diplomatic corps and the civil service. Any institution which can
enlist so wide a range of ability will hold an influential place in
society.

Because almost everybody in western Europe was Catholic the
Church presided over all stages of an individual's life. It baptized
newly-born children, blessed marriages, churched women after
childbirth, administered the last rites to the dying, buried the dead
and prayed for the souls of the faithful departed. The Church also
participated in many of the important public events of secular life:
kings were crowned by bishops; knights received investiture in
a religious ceremony; feudal and legal oaths were administered
by the clergy and were sworn on relics or gospel books; the clergy
of each parish blessed the fields every year in the rogationtide
processions.

Although the average level of religious practice was low and
religious doubt was widespread, these facts were not considered
incompatible with membership of the Church, as nowadays they
tend to be. Everybody in western Europe who was not a Muslim or
a Jew was baptized at birth and received a Catholic funeral when
he died. This minimum of conformity with Catholic practice was
universal. The degree to which men participated in the life of the

Church between the cradle and the grave varied considerably: some people heard Mass every day, while others rarely, if ever, set foot in a church. But to opt out of membership of the Church entirely was almost unheard of.

Similarly, although doubts about particular articles of the faith seem to have been widespread, very few people indeed rejected the Catholic religion in its entirety. One reason for this was that medieval Catholicism was not simply a system of belief, it also presented men with a comprehensive explanation of the nature of the world in which they lived. The Church taught that the universe had been created by God, and explained the evil and imperfection which were visible in it as the consequence of a revolt by the fallen angels, led by Lucifer, who made perpetual war against the Almighty and marred His creation in the process. This world picture included a comprehensive view of human history, which began in the Garden of Eden and led, through the incarnation of Christ, to the Last Judgement. The Church taught that each individual had an immortal soul and was accountable before God for the conduct of his life. His eternal destiny, in Hell, Purgatory or Paradise, would depend on the extent to which he had been willing to receive the grace which Christ offered to all men, of which the Church was the guaranteed depository. Not everybody was equally well informed about all these teachings; many people were sceptical about particular points in them; but virtually nobody challenged the overall picture of the universe which the Church presented, for the good reason that there was no alternative model available to them. The acceptance, albeit with some reservations, of a Christian world picture in which the Church held a central place, necessarily entailed the acceptance in some degree of the ministrations of the Church. Some people might be willing to live without them, but very few would wilfully die without them.

The appeal of the Church

The world picture which the Church offered appealed to human reason: the desire which people have to make sense of the universe around them. But reason is only part of the human personality, and the Church owed its power also to its ability to cope with men's irrational fears. In part these stemmed from an awareness, which we all share, of the powerful forces which exist in the subconscious mind; but this was accompanied by a fear of seemingly irrational forces at work in the natural order. Such fears were fully justified, since medieval people had only a very imperfect control over their environment. The Christian Middle Ages regarded these psychological and natural phenomena as the work of supernatural forces of evil which were trying to gain control of the world. This was, of course, merely the rationalization of an attitude far older than Christianity.

To guard against such evils men looked to the clergy who were trained in spiritual combat. With the judicious use of the relics of the saints, holy water, ceremonies of exorcism, processions of the Blessed Sacrament and other suitable rites priests could rout the forces of evil and avert psychological and natural disasters which threatened to overwhelm individuals or communities. Few people in the Middle Ages, however lapsed or assailed by doubt they might be, liked being without the services of a priest which they might call upon at need, just as few modern people like living for any length of time in a place which is inaccessible to a doctor.

Medieval western society was based on religious assumptions, and the Church was taken entirely for granted by everybody. Like or dislike of the institutional Church, fervour or indifference in religious practice, were irrelevant in such a society, where the Church was regarded as a fundamental part of life, not as an optional extra. A society of this kind is not a favourable milieu for the growth of some kinds of heresy. This is not equally true of all kinds of heresy. A religious society naturally produces some men who dissent on intellectual grounds from some received point of doctrine. Medieval western society produced its fair share of academic heretics of this kind, but most of their speculations were so technical that they did not attract either a popular following or popular animosity, and it was normally left to their fellow theologians to convict them of error and force them to recant. There was another type of heretic, who wanted to reform the institutional Church. Some of the reforms such men proposed were radical: Tanchelm, for example, preached at Antwerp in the early twelfth century that holy orders were unnecessary and that Holy Communion was not an effective channel of grace. Such men, though understandably harassed by the clergy, often attracted a large lay following, since what they appeared to be offering was an improved and purified version of the existing Church, and there was general agreement that the Church was in need of reform.

The heretics who excited popular hostility were those who advocated that the Church as men knew it should be abolished altogether, because it was a false Church, inspired by the devil and not by God. All societies have limits to what they are prepared to tolerate, otherwise they would be anarchies. The limits of medieval western toleration were reached when radical attacks of this kind were made on the Church to which everybody belonged and in whose values they all to some extent shared. The heretics no doubt thought that they were simply attacking the Church, but they

were, in fact, attacking the entire social order of which the Church
formed an indivisible part. No society which has faith in its own
values will tolerate public criticism of that kind, and from its first
appearance this sort of radical heresy was treated not merely as an
error but as a crime.

2
The growth of heresy up to 1215

The Cathars

The most important group of radical heretics to trouble the peace of the Church in the central Middle Ages was the Cathars, whom Pope Innocent III likened, in the words of *The Song of Songs*, to 'the little foxes that spoil the vines'. The Cathars, who shared the pope's taste for the allegorical interpretation of scripture, considered themselves the lost sheep of the house of Israel whom Christ had come to save. Their name derives from the Greek word *katharoi*, meaning the pure, for they claimed to hold the Christian faith in its pristine form. It has now been established beyond doubt that they were a western branch of the Bogomils, a dualist sect which originated in Bulgaria in the tenth century. This was known at the time, and Old French writers sometimes referred to them as *bougres*, thus enriching the vernacular with a new term of abuse. In its modern sense the term is singularly ill suited to describe one of the most high-minded groups of people that western society has ever seen.

The Cathars differed from other groups of heretics in that they already had a defined corpus of doctrine, a tradition of Biblical exegesis, a uniform liturgy and rule of life and an ecclesiastical organization before they entered western Europe. They did not depend, as most heresies did, on the forceful personality of a leader and they were thus more resistant to persecution. They used an entirely Christian vocabulary and accepted the New Testament as divinely inspired, but it is nevertheless debatable whether they may justly be considered as part of the Christian tradition at all, for they denied what all other Christians have regarded as the first article of their faith, belief in one God, 'maker . . . of all things visible and invisible'. Although there were significant doctrinal differences between different groups of them, all Cathars were agreed that the phenomenal world had been brought into being either by an evil god, or by a fallen demiurge, against the wishes of the Good God. They believed that the souls of men, created by the Good God, were imprisoned in bodies of flesh by the evil principle and were doomed to an eternal round of reincarnation; while some

at least of them believed that all warm-blooded creatures had souls
of equal dignity with those of men and shared in the process of
reincarnation with them.

The Cathars taught that Christ, whom they recognized in some
sense as the son of the Good God, had come to release imprisoned
souls by founding a church to which He confided His teaching and
the one sacrament of salvation. That church was the Cathar
church; the teaching was that of the New Testament as interpreted
by the Cathar church; and the sacrament was baptism in the spirit
by the laying-on of hands, which the Cathars called the *consolamentum,* or the comforting. This sacrament was administered
only to fully instructed adults or to the dying, and only those who
had received it were members of the church. Such men and women
were known as the perfect and, as became their vocation, they had,
in so far as was possible, to break all ties with the world, which
they held to be totally evil. They renounced all property, all sexual
activities including marriage, all social ties, and placed themselves
totally at the disposal of the Cathar church. They were required
solemnly to undertake to abstain from eating meat and all other
animal products, such as milk, eggs and cheese, and never, even if
in danger of death, to tell a lie, to swear an oath, or to take the life of
a man or a warm-blooded beast. The Cathars had bishops who
ruled over territorial dioceses, each of which was subdivided into
smaller units presided over by deacons. They were implacable in
their hostility to the Catholic Church which, they taught, was a
counterfeit church, founded by the Devil to delude men with false
hopes of salvation. Catharism thus presented a coherent and
radical alternative to orthodox Christianity.

The presence of Cathars in western Europe is first securely
attested at Cologne in 1143. It used to be thought that some earlier
outbreaks of heresy, which contemporary writers labelled Mani-
chaean, were isolated examples of Catharism and, although recent
scholarship has rightly emphasized that there is insufficient
evidence to determine the precise nature of these early heresies, I
incline to think that the older view may well be true. Certainly such
movements had much in common with Catharism: they were
ascetic, world renouncing and whole-hearted in their rejection of
the established Church. If they were not expressions of Catharism
in its fully fledged form, they were at least, I think, offshoots of
Bogomilism in its more primitive form.

The beginnings of heresy

The Church was singularly ill equipped to deal with heresy when it
first became a serious problem in the west. Half a millennium had

passed since the collapse of the Roman Empire and during that time western society had become barbarized: its economic life had been disrupted; its urban centres had become largely depopulated; and it had been subjected to recurrent and wide ranging invasions. The circumstances of life in the west during that period were not conducive to speculative thought. Religious doubt, of course, persisted throughout this time, and there were also some isolated outbreaks of heresy which tended to collapse when their leaders died: such matters were an irritant to the Church, but they were not serious problems.

This period of ecclesiastical tranquillity ended in c. AD 1000. By that time the last barbarian invasions, those of the Magyars and Vikings, had ended and European society was becoming more stable and prosperous than it had been for centuries. Communications became easier, a revival of scholarship began to take place, there was greater opportunity for speculation, and outbreaks of heresy became common. Apart from a brief gap in the second half of the eleventh century, when the papacy placed itself at the head of a movement for Church reform and presumably attracted the support of the devout who might otherwise have joined dissident groups, religious dissent has been a normal part of western European life ever since.

As was noted in the last chapter, medieval heresy took many forms. Academic theologians, like Peter Abelard, who sought to formulate orthodox theology in current philosophical terms, sometimes fell into heresy. In the early period at least they were not a serious problem, except, perhaps, to the other theologians who had to refute them, because their intentions were not heretical and they did not attract a popular following. Other movements, which aimed at reforming the Church in a more or less radical way, were more of a problem to the authorities, but since, with one exception, they depended on the personality of individual charismatic leaders, their influence was limited and they tended to collapse when their leaders died.

The sole exception to this general rule was Waldensianism, which has the distinction of being the only medieval dissenting movement to have survived until the present day. Because it was later persecuted by the Inquisition it merits some detailed consideration in this work. Its founder, Waldo, or Valdes, was a rich merchant of Lyons who in 1173 embraced a life of apostolic poverty and gathered a group of followers whom he encouraged in vernacular Bible reading and evangelical preaching. He did not dispute any point of Catholic doctrine, but the pastoral activities of his followers brought them into conflict with the archbishop of Lyons. Pope Alexander III, to whom the case was referred, found

Waldo completely orthodox in doctrine, but insisted that his followers must have a license to preach from their diocesan bishop. When that permission was refused, the Waldensians went into schism and subsequently evolved their own ordained ministry and began to diverge from the traditional faith of the Roman Church. But, like the Protestant reformed churches with whom they entered into communion in the sixteenth century, the Waldensians were in substantial agreement with Catholics about many, though not all, of the central doctrines of the Christian faith. They survived the death of their founder because their organization gave them a stability which other similar reform-minded groups had lacked, and they initially flourished particularly in southern France and northern Italy, although they also founded some missions in other parts of Europe. Perhaps because they were so close to traditional Catholicism, the Waldensians aroused no popular animosity.

This hostility was reserved for groups of radical heretics, whose beliefs were like those of the Cathars. The earliest case of this kind that is known in any detail is that of some canons of Orleans, who were brought to trial on charges of heresy in 1022. When the bishop of Beauvais, who was interrogating them, asked whether they believed that everything had been created *ex nihilo* by God, they replied:

You may spin stories in that way to those who have earthly wisdom and believe the fictions of carnal men scribbled on animal skins. To us, however, who have the law written upon the heart by the Holy Spirit . . . in vain do you spin out superfluities and things inconsistent with the divinity.
(Paul of Chartres, translated in W.L. Wakefield and A.P. Evans, *Heresies of the High Middle Ages,* New York and London, 1969, p. 81.)

The trial was conducted by clergy in the presence of Robert the Pious, king of France. The accused held high office in the Church, and one of them had been the queen's confessor, and the king reacted to these revelations in much the same spirit as an American president might do if he discovered that a Senate committee was packed with members of the Mafia. He ordered that those who would not recant should be unfrocked and suffer death by burning. This was the first occasion on which heresy was treated as a capital offence in western Europe in the Middle Ages and it created the atrocious precedent for condemning unrepentant heretics to death at the stake. It is significant that this sentence was pronounced by the king of France, not recommended to him by the clergy who were conducting the trial.

This was not an isolated case. In c.1028 Bishop Aribert of Milan discovered a similar group of heretics at the castle of Monforte and arrested them. He and his clergy spent a long time trying to convert them to orthodoxy, but the people of Milan finally took matters into their own hands and, despite the bishop's protests, burnt those heretics who refused to recant. Almost a century later, in 1114, a group of world-renouncing heretics were brought to trial by the bishop of Soissons. He found them guilty, and went to ask the advice of a church council, which was meeting at Beauvais, about how to treat them, but during his absence the people of Soissons, fearing that the clergy would be too lenient, broke into the prison, dragged the heretics out and burnt them. The Cathars who were found at Cologne in 1143 were treated in exactly the same way: the mob seized them and burnt them against the wishes of the clergy who were conducting their trial. Unlike the canons of Orleans, these later groups of proto-Cathars and Cathars were, for the most part, not distinguished in rank or public office, but they aroused intense feelings of fear and hatred among the mass of the people because they dissociated themselves completely from all the values on which society was based.

Attitudes to heresy

The Church did not at this stage approve of the death penalty for heresy and when it remained in control of a heresy trial was lenient in its punishment even of extreme offenders. Thus when the Breton heretic, Eon de l'Étoile, was brought before Pope Eugenius III at the council of Rheims in 1148 and declared, 'I am Eon who shall come to judge the quick and the dead and the world by fire', he was merely sentenced to imprisonment.

But lay rulers might justly have complained that the Church was very difficult to please in this regard. In areas where they co-operated in the suppression of heresy they were accused of acting too harshly, but in areas where they failed to co-operate the Church was scandalized. This was the case in southern France and Lombardy, where Catharism spread rapidly in the second half of the twelfth century. In southern France political power was fragmented, and because the political and ecclesiastical divisions did not correspond very closely it was difficult for the lay authorities to co-operate effectively with the Church in the suppression of heresy. There was a different problem in Lombardy, where the communes, jealous of their independence, were unwilling to weaken their autonomy by allowing the Church to prosecute some of their citizens. In both areas Catharism grew virtually unhindered and Waldensianism also spread there.

Within a generation of the arrival of the first Cathars the people of Languedoc and Lombardy had found that the heretics were not a threat to their society at all. Catholic polemicists were quick to point out the logical consequences of Catharism on a social level: the Cathars were pacifists and their presence would weaken the power of rulers to wage just wars; the Cathars refused to take oaths, and this would undermine the whole fabric of tenurial and legal structures; while the Cathars' abhorrence of sex would, if generally adopted, depopulate whole regions. These fears were found, in practice, to be groundless, because although many people admired the holy lives led by the Cathar elect and believed the explanation which they gave about the nature of evil, few were prepared to emulate them and embrace the austere life of the perfect. Moreover, the Cathars themselves were rigorously selective in the admission of postulants to full membership of their church. Yet in Cathar belief only those who had been consoled were members of the church and were bound by its rules. An unconsoled Cathar believer might behave as he chose: he might marry and beget children, own property, take part in war, swear oaths, eat meat, and even take part in Catholic worship. This did not disconcert Catholic apologists, who promptly claimed that Catharism was subversive of public morality, since the Cathars encouraged their believers to reject Catholic moral standards, but put nothing in their place. In practice, since social pressures seem to be more influential than ethical codes in determining public morality, such criticisms were misplaced, and the morality of Cathar believers was not notably different from that of their Catholic neighbours.

Indeed, the very ordinariness of Cathar believers was the chief dissuasive from persecuting them in Languedoc and Lombardy once they had become established there. Whereas in northern Europe people were frightened by these strange religious fanatics, who condemned the whole society in which they lived and the religious system in which it was grounded, it was not possible for people in southern Europe to react in the same extravagant way towards their widowed mothers or next-door neighbours who became Cathar believers. A southern French Catholic knight, when asked by Bishop Fulk of Toulouse why men like himself did not prosecute heretics, explained:

We cannot do it. We have grown up with them, we are closely related to some of them, and we can see what respectable lives they lead.
(William of Puylaurens. *Chronique, 1203—1275*, ed. and trans.

J. Duvernoy, *Sources d'histoire médiéval*, Paris, 1976, pp. 50—1.)

The perfected Cathars were a different matter, since by virtue of their profession they did opt out of all social obligations. But they were never numerous and were no more difficult for society to assimilate than a sudden increase in Carthusian vocations would have been. By the end of the twelfth century southern Europe had learned that a plurality of religious confessions is not subversive of social good order, and Catholics, Cathars and Waldensians all enjoyed freedom of worship and of speech throughout Languedoc and Lombardy.

Had Catharism been confined to a minority group of *perfecti*, and had most believers never been received into their church, the Roman curia might have been less alarmed by the fact that it was tolerated. The Cathars, however, were willing to administer the *consolamentum* to dying believers, and this practice became quite common. It was said, for example, in the early thirteenth century that few people in the villages of Lanta, Caraman and Verfeil in the Lauragais died without being hereticated. This was not a problem to the secular authorities: dying men have few contributions to make to society at large. The Church, however, could not view this phenomenon with the same detachment.

The Church authorities in general, and the popes in particular, disapproved of the toleration of heresy in southern Europe for precisely the same reason as they frowned upon the summary execution of heretics in northern Europe. The pope, as vicar of Christ, was answerable before God for the souls of everybody in his charge, and their salvation depended on their dying in a state of grace. Profession of heresy at the time of death made this impossible. We are now so used, in the present climate of oecumenism, to clergymen of different confession being politely tolerant of the dogmatic issues that divide them, that it is easy to forget how recent a development this is. Until about 50 years ago the Christian Church in all its main branches had never regarded the toleration of doctrinal error as a virtue. The Church's Founder, it is true, may have taken a more liberal view of diversity of opinion, but, if so, few of His followers shared it. St Paul admonished Titus:

If a man disputes what you teach, then after a first and second warning, have no more to do with him. You will know that a man of that sort has already lapsed and condemned himself as a sinner.
(Titus, ch. 3, vv. 10—11.)

All the Fathers held the same views and the medieval Catholic Church therefore had unanimous apostolic and patristic support in regarding heresy as a very grave sin indeed.

The Church condemned equally all varieties of heresy: that of the academic theologians, the popular reformers and the dualist Cathars. Offenders were brought before the Church courts and were urged to recant: if they did so there was no further problem, although they might be given a penance as they would have been for any other kind of sin. In the case of those who refused to recant the Church had, for a long time, no agreed policy. Bishop Wazo of Liège, a learned canon lawyer, when consulted by the bishop of Châlons-sur-Marne about an outbreak of heresy in his diocese in the 1040s, counselled moderation. Those who refused to recant should be debarred from the sacraments, but not otherwise harassed, and Wazo concluded:

> Although Christian piety despises these tenets . . . nevertheless, in emulation of our Saviour . . . we are commanded for a time to bear with such things in some measure.
> (Wakefield and Evans, *op. cit.*, p. 91)

Excommunication did not prove a very effective deterrent when applied to heretics, part of whose offence usually consisted in denying the validity of Catholic sacraments. The lay solution of burning unrepentant heretics may have had a deterrent effect on their supporters, but it did not satisfy the Church because dead men are beyond the powers of the most eloquent apologist to convert. The same was also true, of course, of Cathar believers who were hereticated on their deathbeds. The Church did not wish heretics to be killed while they were unrepentant, or to be tolerated and infect others with their wrong belief. A compromise solution to this problem began to emerge in the course of the twelfth century.

Canon law

This came about as a consequence of the revival of the study of civil and canon law which was part of the complex intellectual movement known as the twelfth-century renaissance. The civil lawyers used as their fundamental text the law code of Justinian, in which heresy was equated with treason and was punishable by death. At about the same time canon lawyers found in the works of some of the Fathers, notably St Augustine and St Leo the Great, the opinion that the secular authority might be invoked to coerce obdurate heretics who would not be moved by argument. Gratian in his commentary on canon law accepted that the state had coercive powers in regard to heretics and inferred that a contumacious heretic had no right to property and that his life could be forfeited also, provided that this was done by lawful authority and for the common good. Gratian's work had no statutory force, but it was very influential because it was prescribed reading for all students of canon law.

Thus in the course of the twelfth century, as heresy became more widespread, the attitude of civil and canon lawyers towards it became convergent. The relative spheres of Church and state in the work of suppressing heresy were not defined until 1184, when Pope Lucius III issued the bull *Ad abolendam* with the concurrence of the emperor Frederick Barbarossa. This decreed that bishops should visit places in their dioceses where heresy was said to exist and seek out heretics on the testimony of local witnesses of proven orthodoxy. Such heretics should be tried in the bishop's court and, if they proved contumacious, handed over to the secular ruler for punishment. The nature of that punishment is not specified, beyond provision that vassals suspected of heresy should be deprived of their fiefs unless they could prove their innocence. Innocent III specified the penalty for heresy more precisely in the bull *Vergentis in senium* of 1199: the lands of proven heretics were to be confiscated by secular lords, without right of appeal, and without respect to the rights of Catholic heirs. This legislation did not envisage the use of the death penalty, since the pope stipulated that heretics who later repented might receive their lands back again.

This legislation was not entirely effective: in northern Europe lay people still tended to regard burning as the natural way of dealing with Cathars, while in Languedoc and Lombardy the repressive legislation was not enacted at all. The problem in southern Europe seemed particularly urgent, because heresy was visibly spreading there at a rapid rate and in the view of the Church an unacceptably large number of people were being damned through dying in the wrong faith. Innocent III, who became pope in 1198, began to take matters in hand, concentrating his efforts on Languedoc where, for political reasons, intervention was easier. He began by exhorting local rulers to bring the heretics to trial and, when that had no effect, he organized intensive preaching tours of the area under the auspices of the Cistercian Order, in an attempt to combat heresy by persuasion. This peaceful initiative came to an abrupt end in 1208 when a papal legate was assassinated, it was supposed with the complicity of the count of Toulouse, which led Innocent III to launch the Albigensian Crusade against Languedoc in 1209.

The Albigensian crusade

This war, which dragged on inconclusively for 20 years until the
French crown intervened and assumed direct rule over most of the
territory, was not primarily intended to extirpate heresy. Its main
purpose was to transfer the lands of southern France to rulers who
were orthodox, and who would therefore, it was hoped, co-operate
with the Church in the suppression of Catharism. But the majority
of crusaders came from northern Europe and reacted to heretics
when they encountered them as they did in their homeland, by
burning them. Initially, at least, professed Cathars were not difficult to identify because they wore distinctive dress. The crusaders
took this as sufficient evidence of guilt and made no attempt to try
them. Indeed, when the pope's legate insisted that professed
Cathars captured at Minerve in 1210 should at least be given the
opportunity to recant before they were executed, he met with considerable opposition. On that occasion 140 heretics were burnt at
one time, and such expressions of crusader zeal remained quite
common until the perfect became more discreet and adopted lay
dress.

In practice, therefore, there was a dichotomy of aim between
clergy and laity about the treatment of heretics until the early
thirteenth century. The Church authorities were concerned to
check the spread of heresy and to convert the heretics, whereas lay
people were either content to give them complete freedom, or
anxious to take the law into their own hands and to lynch them. It
was not a situation the Church could responsibly allow to continue. Legally, heresy was a crime which only the Church had the
technical expertise to identify; morally the Church was accountable to God for the souls of all the faithful, even of those who had
fallen into error, and it could not discharge that duty if they were
dead. The Albigensian Crusade, with its many summary execu-
tions, highlighted this problem. Lynching then reached unprece-
dented proportions. Almost certainly more heretics were burnt
without trial during the first five years of the crusade than had
been executed in the previous two centuries. Innocent III had been
trained as a canon lawyer and legislation about heresy was one
of the matters he placed on the agenda of the Fourth Lateran
Council, summoned to meet in 1215.

3
The foundation of the Inquisition

The Lateran Council of 1215

The Fourth Lateran Council which opened in Rome in November 1215 was the largest assembly of its kind in the history of the Christian Church. Over 400 bishops and 800 abbots were present, together with representatives of prelates who did not attend in person and delegates sent by the Western emperor, the Latin emperor of Constantinople, and the kings of England, France, Aragon, Hungary, Cyprus and Jerusalem. It was thus widely representative of the whole of Latin Christendom and for that reason its enactments were likely to command general assent.

One of the Council's main concerns was the problem of heresy. It issued a detailed formulation of orthodox belief, which not merely reiterated the traditional faith of the Church, but also listed, clause by clause, the ways in which that faith was erroneously interpreted by heretics, particularly by Cathars. The Council also imposed upon all adult Catholics of both sexes the obligation of making confession to their parish priests and receiving Holy Communion once a year at Eastertide. It is generally thought that this was intended to check the spread of heresy, by singling out convinced dissenters from the mass of Catholics who were luke-warm in the practice of their faith.

The Council also codified and augmented the existing heresy laws. Canon Three enacted that all heretics who refused to recant and to accept the creed as defined by the Council should be excommunicated and handed over to the secular authorities for punishment. The nature of this punishment was not specified, but it was decreed that such people should forfeit their property, which should be confiscated by lay rulers, except in the case of convicted clergy, whose property should be given to the Church. Those who were suspected, but not convicted, of heresy should be required to prove their innocence by compurgation: that is, they should produce a specified number of witnesses who would be prepared to swear a solemn oath that the suspects were orthodox. If a suspect failed to do this within a year he would incur automatic excommunication and be treated as a proven heretic. All public authorities

31

should be required to swear on oath that they would punish those whom the Church declared to be heretics. Secular rulers who refused to comply with this requirement should be excommunicated and if they refused to make their peace with the Church within a year their lands might be seized by their Catholic neighbours, though the rights of the principal lord must be safeguarded in such cases. Those who took part in just wars of this kind should enjoy the same spiritual privileges as attached to crusaders to the Holy Land. Heretical believers, together with those who, while not necessarily suspected of holding heretical opinions, nevertheless offered protection or hospitality or any kind of help to heretics should also be excommunicated and should lose their civil rights unless they were reconciled to the Church within a year. Those rights were defined as the right to hold public office, the right to vote in elections, the right to make a legal will, and the right to inherit property. Those who died while excommunicated for any of the reasons specified should be denied Christian burial and any clergy who defied this ruling should be suspended from office and their cases should be reserved to the judgement of the Holy See. Each bishop, or his archdeacon or some other official, should visit once or twice a year those places in his diocese where heresy was reputed to exist and seek out heretics on the sworn evidence of three or more witnesses of good character. Those accused should be required to undergo canonical compurgation and any who refused to take an oath should, *ipso facto,* be deemed guilty of heresy. Bishops who were lax in the prosecution of heresy would be removed from office by the pope.

It was the hope of the Council that secular rulers would make this canon the basis of their own heresy laws, so that in future Church and state might follow a common code of practice in regard to heresy. Only two countries in western Europe had enacted laws against heresy before this time. One of them was England, and this was surprising because it was the one major state in Europe which had been almost totally free from heresy in this period. However, a group of continental Cathars had been tried by a Church synod at Oxford in the 1160s and, although they had only made one convert, Henry II regarded them as sufficient of a menace not only to merit flogging and branding, but also to warrant the inclusion of a special clause in the Assizes of Clarendon forbidding any of his subjects to associate with them. At the other end of Christendom, in Aragon, Alphonso II decreed in 1194 that heretics should be expelled from his kingdom, and in 1197 his successor, Peter II, ordered that convicted heretics should be burnt. But such formal legislation was uncommon and throughout most of western Europe the repression of heresy was dictated only by custom.

The attempts of the Church after 1215 to persuade secular rulers to enact legislation against heretics in conformity with the rulings of canon law have sometimes been taken as evidence that the papacy was seeking to force tolerant governments to adopt its own coercive policies. This is only partly true, for the majority of secular princes had used physical coercion to repress heresy since the eleventh century. It is too often forgotten that the Church had stood out against the violent treatment of heretics for almost 200 years, as long a period as separates us from the American Revolution. It is, indeed, arguable that the Church finally came to condone coercion because the attitude of the clergy was shaped by the society in which they lived, which regarded the persecution of heretics as normal.

Enforcement of the heresy laws

The Church received the strongest and most immediate support for the implementation of the canons of the Fourth Lateran Council from Frederick II, Holy Roman Emperor and king of Sicily, whose authority extended in theory over Germany and the whole of Italy, except the States of the Church. At his coronation as emperor in 1220 he incorporated the canon law enactments against heresy in the laws of the Western Empire and in 1224 he specified the secular penalties for convicted heretics: normally they should be burnt, but, if their lives were spared, they should have their tongues cut out.

Frederick was a complex figure, known to his contemporaries as *immutator mundi*, the transformer of the world. Some of his views were certainly revolutionary: in his scientific writings he was, unlike most of his contemporaries, willing to reject the authority of classical scholars, notably Aristotle, when it conflicted with his own observation; when he regained Jerusalem from the Saracens he allowed the Muslims to keep control of the Temple area and to perform their devotions in public there. Such attitudes, which shocked many of his contemporaries, have led some modern scholars to treat him as a Renaissance prince born out of time and they, in their turn, have been shocked by the harshness of his heresy laws and have blamed the papacy for coercing him to adopt them. Since those laws exceeded the wishes of the Church in their severity and since Frederick was at open war with the papacy throughout much of his reign, such an explanation is not very convincing. In his attitude to the imperial office Frederick II was very conservative: he spent most of his life fighting to make the Holy Roman Empire a political reality, and he naturally detested heresy, which he regarded as an affront to Almighty God, whose representative on earth in secular affairs he claimed to be.

The other chief ruler in western Europe was the king of France. Ever since 1022, when Robert the Pious had burnt the canons of Orleans, the Capetians had been assiduous in their suppression of heresy, and in 1226 Louis VIII enacted that supporters of heretics should be debarred from public office and have their lands confiscated. In 1233 James I of Aragon also incorporated many of the provisions of the Fourth Lateran Council in the laws of his kingdom. Thus within 20 years of the Council the secular authorities in all those countries of western Europe in which heresy was at all common had sanctioned the enforcement of the Church's decrees against heresy.

When Gregory IX became pope in 1227 all the necessary preparations seemed to have been made for a concerted attack by the ecclesiastical and secular authorities against heresy. Yet in a society like that of medieval western Europe, where no state had either a police force or a standing army, there was a great disjunction between law enactment and law enforcement. Two problems hindered the enforcement of the heresy laws. First, rulers often had only imperfect control within their states. This was particularly true of the greatest western ruler, Frederick II, whose authority was weak outside the Sicilian kingdom and specially weak in Lombardy, where heresy was strong, but where many of the communes were opposed to him. The other problem occurred in states like Capetian France, where royal power was more of a reality, for there heresy had been driven underground as a result of persecution and was difficult to detect.

In areas like Lombardy, where some of the communes refused to co-operate with the Church in the prosecution of heresy, unusual steps had to be taken to enforce canon law, and consideration of this is best deferred to a later chapter. But in countries where the ecclesiastical and civil authorities were united in their desire to prosecute heretics the difficulty remained of identifying them. The imposition of Easter duties proved to be of little help in this regard, particularly in dealing with Cathars. For believers were free to conform, but attached no significance to doing so, while the perfect discovered, in case of need, a loophole in the regulations. It was open to any Catholic to inform his parish priest that he had not committed any sin in the past year worthy of confession and this was difficult to disprove. There were also few priests who would force a parishioner to make his communion at Easter if he said that he considered that he was unworthy to do so. On occasion Cathar *perfecti* used these subterfuges without arousing suspicion, though this was, of course, only possible in an age when the concept of Easter duties was new and unfamiliar.

Inquisition

In such circumstances heretics had to be sought out, and that is the primary sense of inquisition, which means simply inquiry. Such investigations were the responsibility of the bishops, for a bishop was, under the pope, the final authority in his own diocese and cases of heresy were judged in his court. The bull *Ad abolendam* of 1184 had ordered all bishops to make inquisition for heresy and this enactment was reiterated by the Fourth Lateran Council. This system, however, proved a failure. There were many reasons for this. Some, perhaps many, bishops in the thirteenth century were not in the habit of visiting their dioceses for any purpose and would not begin to do so in order to seek out heretics. A few, perhaps, may have been in the position of the bishop of Carcassonne at the time of the Albigensian crusade, who had a mother who was a Cathar *perfecta* and was inhibited from persecuting her fellow believers. Yet even conscientious bishops with no heterodox connections would have found the work of inquisition difficult. If heresy was at all widespread in a diocese it would have been very time-consuming to carry out regular visitations of the affected areas, to examine witnesses and to interrogate suspects. Medieval bishops were not, on the whole, idle men, but their time was occupied very differently from that of their modern successors. Most of them had large estates to manage, many of them had great lordships to govern, and all of them had to deal with a good deal of legal and administrative work which nowadays would be the province of the civil authorities. Such men had little time to spare for hunting down heretics, however desirable in theory they may have considered such work to be.

Because the episcopal inquisition was not working efficiently Blanche of Castile, as regent of France for the young St Louis, ordered royal officials to make inquisition for heresy in 1229, and in 1233 Raymond VII of Toulouse ordered his own officials to do the same in those parts of Languedoc which remained under his personal rule. Some heretics were arrested in this way and were handed over to the Church courts, but on the whole the system did not work well. Lay officials were not trained in theology and could only arrest notorious heretics who were denounced to them: they were powerless to discover concealed heretics, who were numerous.

A third method of inquisition was devised by Cardinal Romanus, papal legate in Languedoc, and enacted by the council of Toulouse in 1229. It was later introduced in a modified form in Aragon by King James I. This consisted in the establishment in every parish of a panel made up of the priest and two or three laymen of known orthodoxy, who should denounce heretics to the bishop. It was very similar to the grand jury of presentment in English law. It freed bishops from the burden of making inquisition, but, like other methods, it was ineffective. The parish priest was usually a local man and his loyalties, like those of his fellow jurors, lay more with the local community, irrespective of its orthodoxy, than with the diocesan authorities. These panels were sworn in, but they did not report.

What the Church needed in order to put its measures against heresy into effect were full-time, professional investigators: men who had a theological training which would enable them to identify heretics, but who had no other duties to perform and who were without local loyalties in the regions where they worked. Pope Gregory IX recognized that such men were to be found in the two new mendicant orders, those of the Dominicans and the Franciscans.

The friars as inquisitors

The Dominican Order seemed particularly well suited to this task for it had been founded specifically to combat Catharism. Its founder, St Dominic Guzman, was a Castilian nobleman and priest who had taken part in the preaching mission in Languedoc in 1206—7 and had become convinced of the need to combat Catharism on its own terms. This involved preaching, which the Cathars considered important but which the Catholic parish clergy neglected, and apostolic poverty, which the Cathar *perfecti* practised, but which was notably absent from the Catholic Church, since even the religious orders, whose members were vowed to individual poverty, possessed great corporate wealth. Dominic stayed in Languedoc during the crusade and gathered round him a number of like-minded priests who came to form the nucleus of the Dominican Order, or, more correctly, the Order of Preachers, which was licensed by Honorius III in 1217. Unlike earlier orders the Dominicans were not allowed to own corporate property except for chapels and priory buildings and their furnishings, and had to beg their daily food (hence they became known as mendicants). The Dominicans received a rigorous training in theology and their vocation was to preach and to hear confessions, for it was the intention of their founder to produce a well-instructed laity which would be less vulnerable to the errors of heretical teachers.

The order grew rapidly and by the time St Dominic died in 1221 it had spread to most of western Europe and was divided into a number of provinces, which owed obedience to the Master General who had no superior but the pope. The Order was exempt from episcopal jurisdiction and its members could be moved from one place to another on the orders of their superiors, unlike the members of older monastic orders who took a vow of stability to a particular house. Such men were clearly well equipped to combat heresy, but it is ironic that the order founded by St Dominic, who was one of the very few people who attempted to convert heretics by reasoned persuasion, should have been entrusted with the work of forcibly suppressing religious dissent.

The medieval Inquisition is quite often described as the Dominican Inquisition, but from the beginning the Franciscans were associated in that work. The use of Franciscans as inquisitors is at first sight surprising. St Francis was a younger contemporary of St Dominic's, his order had been licensed by Innocent III, and by the pontificate of Gregory IX it too was an international order, with provinces all over the western world; it was exempt from the authority of diocesan bishops, and it was administered by a Minister General who was immediately subject to the pope. Like the Dominicans the Franciscans were vowed to corporate poverty and lived by begging; like the Dominicans they also had a vocation to a preaching ministry, but in other ways the two orders did not, in origin, have much in common.

St Francis is often misunderstood because he is associated with sentimental anecdotes, such as preaching to the birds, told of him by some of his early biographers and made popular through the paintings of Giotto. Such views distort the truth. He was inspired by a single ideal: to teach men to live without compromise the life of perfection set forth in the Gospels. It is clearly a matter of regret to some of his non-Catholic biographers that the Church authorities gave him every encouragement in his mission and that he was not, like so many other reformers, driven into schism. The problem did not, in fact, arise, because St Francis had a profound respect for the Church's teaching *magisterium* and for the authority of the hierarchy. He was completely orthodox in doctrine, refused to allow his followers to preach without the license of a parish priest, and refused to claim any privileges for his order. The majority of his followers had been laymen before they made their profession and in his lifetime they were not normally priested. Perhaps the chief difference between St Francis and St Dominic lay in their attitudes to learning, for St Francis saw no place for scholarship, even for theological scholarship, among his friars. Simplicity was the hallmark of the Franciscans, and their founder believed that the teachings of the Gospels would speak for themselves. He did not dispute the value of theological study, but he did not consider it part of the Franciscan vocation.

Even during his lifetime the character of his order began to change and that change was accelerated after his death in 1226. A higher proportion of the friars became priests, some houses of study were opened and, as a result, some Franciscans became trained theologians. It was natural that Pope Gregory IX, who as Cardinal Ugolino had been the chief patron in the curia of the young Franciscan order, should turn to it for help in combatting heresy once it had some members with the right qualifications. The pope did not consider that he was diverting the order from its original function, since he regarded the suppression of error as an integral part of pastoral care.

It was to these new and lively orders that Gregory IX entrusted the work which bishops had proved incapable of doing, that of making inquisition for heresy. They were eminently suited to this task. Their members were trained in theology and therefore qualified to identify heretics; but they were also trained in pastoral work and knew how to talk to ordinary people, which most professional theologians did not. The orders had attracted some of the best intellects among the younger generation of men trained in the universities. The friars were all vowed to individual and corporate poverty and were likely to be impervious to bribes; their orders were directly under the authority of the pope, *nullo medio*; and the friars, unlike earlier inquisitors, could engage in the work of inquisition on a full-time basis.

Initially, at least, the Inquisition staffed by members of the mendicant orders, did not supersede all other forms of inquisition. Episcopal inquisitions continued to function concurrently with it and secular officials continued to make sporadic inquisitions for heresy in some places. In the early days secular clergy were also sometimes associated with the mendicants in their inquisitorial work. But as the new Inquisition proved its effectiveness it came more and more to take over the work of prosecuting heresy and its personnel became exclusively friars.

It should, however, be stressed that only a few members of the Dominican and Franciscan Orders were involved in the work of inquisition. Provincials and ministers in certain areas were required by the pope to second some of their brethren, usually not more than about four, to carry out such duties. The majority of the friars never became inquisitors at all, but carried on with their pastoral work, and it is arguable that they made a greater contribution to the suppression of heresy than their inquisitor brethren. For it was the friars who were responsible in the thirteenth century for the growth of a devout laity which the medieval west had never previously known. Both orders sought to produce better instructed lay people; both encouraged the laity to take a more

active part in the sacramental life of the Church; and both taught
that the full practice of the Christian life was compatible with the
lay state. These measures eroded support for heresy, which had
derived much of its earlier popularity from lay people who, in all
but a technical sense, had been neglected by the Catholic clergy
who had offered them little practical guidance about how to lead
the Christian life. To that extent the work of the Inquisition, which
was entirely negative in its aims and its achievements, cannot be
considered in isolation from the pastoral activities of the mendicant orders which were designed to build up the faith and practice
of lay people.

It is idle to speculate whether the creation of the Inquisition was
a work of supererogation and whether heresy would have declined
in any case as a result of the pastoral work of the mendicant orders.
From the reign of Gregory IX the Inquisition had become an
established part of western society.

4
The interrogation of suspects

The Inquisition was founded primarily to combat Catharism, which the Church regarded as the best-organized and most dangerous of the various heretical movements existing in western Europe in the thirteenth century. Inevitably, because it was the appropriate tribunal, the Inquisition also dealt with any other kinds of heresy that came to its notice, such as Waldensianism, but these groups were not its principal concern. This is made plain in the manuals the inquisitors wrote, in which heresy is equated with Catharism, whereas other dissenting movements are called simply by their own names. In the fourteenth century, when Catharism had virtually collapsed, the Inquisition continued to exist and was used by the authorities for other purposes which were less reputable when judged by its own criteria, such as bringing the Knights Templar to trial. Inquisition procedures had, however, been developed to deal with Catharism, and they must therefore be first examined in that context. The ways in which they were subsequently adapted to meet the requirements of a quite different range of cases which were deemed to be within the competence of the tribunal will be considered in later chapters of this book.

The powers of inquisitors

In theory the powers of inquisitors were extensive. They had jurisdiction over everybody living within the area in which the pope commissioned them to operate, except for diocesan bishops and their officials: until the fourteenth century even papal legates were not, in theory, exempt from their authority. Inquisitors were accountable only to the pope and he alone had the right to excommunicate or suspend them. Their religious superiors in their respective orders had no authority over them in their capacity as inquisitors, and there was great uncertainty throughout the thirteenth century about whether a superior could recall a brother from the work of inquisition and replace him by another member of the order. This was a matter about which successive popes gave conflicting rulings. The inquisitors might receive evidence submitted by anybody, even by people whose testimony was not normally accepted for legal purposes, such as the excommunicate; and wives and husbands were allowed to testify against each other in the courts of the Inquisition.

Nevertheless, these powers which looked so impressive on paper could prove to be quite flimsy in practice. In the first place an inquisitor was totally dependent on the readiness of the secular authorities to co-operate with him. Detailed consideration of this point is best reserved to later chapters, but the general principle needs to be emphasized: whereas it could be assumed that any other criminal court would command the support of secular rulers, no such assumption could be made in the case of the Inquisition. This could inhibit its work, since the inquisitors had no coercive powers of their own. It is true that after 1242 they were allowed to arm the members of their households but this measure was merely intended to give them protection from attack, and the number of armed retainers each was permitted was strictly limited by regional statute: in southern France, for example, it was three.

But perhaps the greatest limitation on the powers of the inquisitors was one which was inherent in the aim of their tribunal: the desire to convert all those convicted of heresy to orthodox belief and to restore them to full membership of the Catholic Church. Other criminal courts had a simpler task, that of establishing the guilt of an accused person and then sentencing him in accordance with the law. The courts of the Inquisition were concerned first with establishing guilt, but secondly with persuading the offender to recant, and only then with passing sentence on him. This is not a subtle distinction: a repentant heretic was never burnt, whereas those who refused to recant normally were. The desire to secure recantations in practice was a severe limitation to the arbitrary exercise by the inquisitors of their very wide powers.

The aim to convert heretics rather than to convict them which characterized the work of the Inquisition may explain why inquisitors were given no training in law. A sound knowledge of theology was essential to enable them to identify heresy and to refute it, but a knowledge of law was not a prerequisite in members of a tribunal who were less concerned to make the punishment fit the crime than, if possible, to persuade the offender to accept a penance commensurate with his sin. The skills which were needed for that purpose were those of the priest, and it was priests from the mendicant orders who undertook this work.

Inquisitorial procedure

Inquisitorial procedure was standardized within 10 years of the inception of the tribunal, and its overall pattern did not change very much throughout the rest of the Middle Ages although some points of detail were modified (these will be noted where appropriate). The first task which confronted an inquisitor was to discover who the offenders were before he could bring them to trial. His normal method was to visit a town or village which was commonly reported to be a centre of heresy. In the early period at least he did not have a very impressive retinue. The inquisitor himself would be dressed in a Dominican or Franciscan habit, and would be accompanied by a notary and two or three trustworthy men who would act as sworn witnesses, and perhaps by a servant to perform domestic duties. On arrival he would, with the help of the parish priest, gather the population together in the church or in the square and preach to them about the sinfulness of heresy. There was no compulsion to be present, although most people probably attended in order to find out what was happening. In the course of his sermon the inquisitor would declare a period of grace, lasting for perhaps a week, during which anybody who had been guilty of heresy, or of associating with heretics, might make a voluntary confession with the assurance that he would only be given a canonical penance however serious his offence had been. The inquisitor urged all men over the age of 14 and women over the age of 12 to avail themselves of this indulgence if they had offended in this way: children below those ages were not, of course, liable to prosecution. It was made plain that anybody who wished to take advantage of the period of grace would only be treated with leniency if they told the full truth about their own involvement in heresy and what they knew about the involvement of others.

The inquisitor then retired to his lodgings and waited. If, as occasionally happened, the community was united in its refusal to co-operate with him, he could either move on to some other place and take no action, or he could require the entire population to give evidence. Although not common, this procedure was sometimes used. In 1245–6 Bernard of Caux and John of St Pierre, the inquisitors of Toulouse, took depositions from some 8,000–10,000 people in that area, calling in whole villages for questioning. Large-scale interrogations of this kind were not, of course, conducted by the inquisitors in person, for, however dedicated they were to their work, two men could not have dealt with interviews on that scale. Depositions were made in the presence of notaries of the court in answer to set questions, and were witnessed and signed in due form. Nowadays such information would be gathered by circulating forms, but such a procedure could not be used in a society where literacy was not common. The inquisitors could examine the depositions made in their absence and recall any witnesses they wished to question further.

The inquisitors did not normally find reticence an obstacle when they asked for volunteers to assist them in their inquiries. They probably devised this method in the first place because as priests they were aware of the extent to which tensions exist in any small community. Some people availed themselves of the period of grace because they were genuinely repentant, or because they were timid, but spite towards and envy of their neighbours seem commonly to have motivated many such witnesses. People who came before the Inquisition of their own accord were likely to be willing to tell all that they knew about their own involvement in heresy and that of others. Their depositions were recorded in due form and legally witnessed. The inquisitors kept their half of the bargain: such witnesses were absolved from excommunication which they had incurred because of their heretical activities and were given canonical penances, usually quite light ones.

No sin was too serious to be forgiven in a willing penitent. If a Cathar *perfectus* spontaneously presented himself to the tribunal, and this, although rare, was not unknown, he received a warm welcome because he could supply more information about heretics than anybody else. He was not merely reconciled to the Church, but was often encouraged to join a mendicant order and, after the necessary training, was seconded to the work of inquisition. Raynier Sacconi, who became Dominican inquisitor in Lombardy in 1252, had previously been not merely a *perfectus* but also an ordained minister in the Cathar church.

With the aid of the depositions made by willing informants the inquisitors were able to compile a list of suspects. They required the evidence of two witnesses before they were able to prosecute, but when this had been obtained the accused could be summoned to appear before them. His attendance was voluntary, but failure to comply was construed as evidence of guilt, and this would lead to his arrest by the secular authorities.

The trial of the accused

The trial was held in camera and the public was not admitted. The only people present were the accused, one or more inquisitors, a notary, who made a record of the deposition, and two or more witnesses, members of the inquisitor's staff, who took no part in the proceedings except to attest the validity of the written deposition. The courtroom was not guarded: there was nothing to prevent an accused man from walking out in the middle of a hearing, except the fear that he would then be treated as guilty.

The suspect was not told the names of his accusers. There was a sound reason for this, although the practice would be difficult to defend in terms of equity. Informers were not popular, and if their names became known they were likely to become the victims of a vendetta conducted by the families of the people they had denounced. This happened in the early period, in connection with the episcopal inquisition, and Pope Gregory IX therefore ruled that inquisitors should not reveal the names of accusers. Nevertheless, inquisitors were aware that some accusations might be inspired by malice, and they tried to guard against this by asking each suspect whether anybody bore him mortal enmity. If in his reply he named one of his accusers, he was required to call witnesses to prove that enmity really did exist, and if he succeeded in doing so the case against him was dismissed. Indeed, the accuser might then find himself in serious trouble, because bearing false witness before the Inquisition was a crime which, in theory at least, was as serious as heresy itself. Except in this one instance, the accused was not allowed to call witnesses in his own defence.

Technically an accused man or woman could be represented by a lawyer. In fact this never happened because no lawyer was willing to incur the penalties attaching to those who defended heretics. A lawyer found guilty on that score would lose his right to practise and therefore his livelihood. This would not happen, of course, if his client was acquitted, but the risk was too great for any lawyer to be willing to venture it.

The moral revulsion which is frequently expressed about the Inquisition and its methods is often misplaced in emphasis. An impression is given that the inquisitors treated all degrees of involvement with heresy as equally culpable and punished them accordingly, so that, for example, a woman who had once out of curiosity accompanied a friend to a Cathar meeting would be treated as severely as a lifelong believer who was totally devoted to the cause of heresy. The inquisitors were not fanatics in that sense: they were aware of the pressures which, in a small community, made some degree of social intercourse and perhaps even of religious contact between Catholics and heretics inevitable. They were less interested in formal breaches of canon law than in the willingness of offenders to co-operate with the Church authorities in extirpating heresy. It was in this area that conflicts of loyalty could most easily develop between the inquisitors and the accused, for tolerance of a diversity of religious opinions, which is a social virtue, was, in the view of the inquisitors and of the law which they represented, a sin, which might have been venial in origin, but which, if persisted in, became very grave indeed.

It is, perhaps, worth making the point that in theory a suspect could be acquitted. Of course, when whole districts were called in for questioning the majority of people were found innocent: but they were not suspects, merely witnesses called upon to assist the tribunal in its work. If a suspect, delated by two witnesses, claimed to be innocent, he was not allowed to call witnesses in his own defence or to have expert legal aid. The inquisitors had, therefore, to decide between his own unverifiable assertions and those of his accusers which were equally incapable of proof. In the early days of the Inquisition it was reasonable to assume that very few people indeed could have been free from some illicit degree of association with heretics in the kind of community the tribunal was investigating, so that any suspect who claimed that he had never had any contact with heresy at all would be straining the inquisitors' credulity. In such circumstances acquittals were very rare, but they were not completely unknown.

If an accused man admitted his guilt but was willing to co-operate fully with the tribunal, there was a high probability that he would be given a canonical penance, though a more severe one than he would have received had he made a voluntary submission. His deposition would be read over to him, and he would be required to sign it or to authenticate it in some way. He was then released, but sentence was not passed until the inquisitors had completed all their investigations in a particular locality.

The inquisitors seem to have been scrupulously honest in record-ing depositions. It would have been very easy for them to persuade an illiterate suspect to sign a false statement incriminating himself or others. Yet although they were accused by their enemies of many malpractices that of falsifying written evidence was not one of them. Had they been primarily concerned, as they are some-times represented as being, with convicting suspects, this would have been an obvious way of dealing with cases where they were held up by insufficient evidence. But they were principally con-cerned to convert those who were guilty of heresy and only a true confession would serve their purpose in that regard.

Not all interrogations were straightforward. A suspect might be willing to confess his own involvement in heresy and express a wish to recant, and yet refuse to give information to the inquisitors which would implicate his family or friends. In addition, there were suspects who admitted their guilt, asked to be reconciled to the Church, and gave the tribunal information about people, but whose sincerity the inquisitors doubted, because they believed that their repentance was motivated by fear. It was considered likely that, given the opportunity, such people would relapse into heresy. This indicates how subjective some of the Inquisition's decisions were bound to be. Repentance through fear is not a response which is capable of legal definition: its recognition involves making a character judgement. As priests belonging to mendicant orders, and therefore trained specially in the work of hearing confessions, inquisitors were better professionally qualified than most of their contemporaries to assess motives.

The disclosure of information

The court had the right to detain for further questioning those whom it considered unco-operative or insincere. They were remanded in prisons belonging to the Inquisition. Such people were not technically under arrest, but were, as we should now say, 'aiding the inquisitors in their inquiries'. They had to report voluntarily to the prison, although failure to do so would be taken as evidence of guilt, but they could be allowed out on bail at the inquisitors' discretion. Applications for bail were commonly granted and willingness to stand bail for a prisoner did not make a man liable to prosecution as a defender of heretics.

People who are unfamiliar with the Inquisition usually associate it with the free use of torture, yet for the first 20 years of its existence the Inquisition did not possess coercive powers of that kind. They were granted to it by Pope Innocent IV in 1252 in his bull *Ad extirpanda*, which gave permission for obdurate suspects to be tortured provided that this did not cause mutilation, effusion of blood, or death. It is difficult to determine how often such methods were used in the thirteenth century: Douais claimed that there were only three instances of the use of torture in the southern French records for this period, but this may merely indicate that the inquisitors did not record its use. It seems doubtful how far the tribunal found it necessary to use torture when dealing with most of its suspects, since it had ample opportunity to inspire fear by other means. On the other hand, had the inquisitors not wished to torture their prisoners on occasion they would have had no need to ask the holy see to grant them this faculty at all.

Obdurate heretics, who might be tortured under the terms of Innocent IV's legislation, were not those who refused to recant, but those who were suspected of refusing to disclose information. There was, however, another type of suspect who proved a great problem to the inquisitors. These were people who professed their willingness to co-operate with the tribunal, but who had perfected the art of equivocation. They never lied, apparently believing it to be a sin to do so, but were quite prepared to tell the truth in ways which would mislead the court. To judge from law reports, people of similar temperament still react in much the same way in modern courts. Their ethical stance is opaque to those who do not share it, but their technique can be highly effective. Bernard Gui, a very experienced inquisitor who held office in Toulouse in the early fourteenth century, was clearly exasperated by suspects of this kind. He complained how, when asked, for example, about their belief in the Church, they replied by asking the inquisitor what he believed. Receiving an orthodox answer they said 'I believe it too', meaning by this that they believed that the inquisitor believed it. In one way such sophistry did not help the suspect, since the Inquisition could detain him indefinitely for further questioning, but it did prevent the tribunal from securing either his conversion or his conviction.

Cathar *perfecti* scorned to act in such a fashion. They could not be summoned to appear before the Inquisition, because in the time of persecution they lived in hiding, but inquisitors sometimes discovered their whereabouts in the course of their examinations, and ordered the secular authorities to arrest them. If apprehended the *perfecti* were imprisoned and brought out for questioning. Since it was part of their profession never to lie in any circumstances, they made no attempt to conceal their beliefs. Inquisitors who wrote manuals for the guidance of less experienced colleagues warned them not to ask leading questions at the beginning of the examination of a *perfectus*, since he would give truthful answers and the interrogation would be ended, whereas a more subtle approach might elicit information which the tribunal would find useful. The *perfecti* impressed even their enemies by their steadfastness: they almost never recanted, and faced death without fear, assured of their salvation.

When the Inquisition examined a suspect they asked questions which ranged over the whole of his life. In the case of an elderly person the resulting deposition could, on occasion, span almost 70 years. Inevitably, much of the evidence contained in such statements related to the heretical activities of people who had died. The inquisitors were interested in establishing the guilt of the dead, because severe penalties attached in canon law to their heirs, even if they were acknowledged to be good Catholics. The dead could not be interrogated, but they could be convicted. To initiate proceedings the evidence of two or more accusers was required, as in the case of the living, and it was then necessary to determine whether the suspect had died in communion with the Catholic Church. Witnesses, who were normally the heirs of the dead man or woman, were called to give evidence. If they could establish that the accused had received the last rites the case usually had to be abandoned, since, whatever his degree of involvement with heresy might have been, this was evidence of his final repentance. Such evidence could only be challenged if it could be proved that the dying man had been hereticated subsequent to his anointing. Cases of this were not unknown, for a dying Cathar believer sometimes sought to safeguard the rights of his heirs by sending for the parish priest, to whose ministrations he attached no significance, but afterwards called in a Cathar *perfectus* to console him in accordance with his own convictions. In the case of heretics who had died before the persecution began and had seen no reason to dissimulate their faith no defence could be offered by their heirs. The difficult cases to decide were those which concerned people who had died suddenly without there being any opportunity to receive the last rites, and the inquisitors then had to weigh the evidence of the accusers against that of the dead person's heirs.

The procedures of the tribunal made the work of a conscientious inquisitor very difficult. In a normal court of law the prosecution witnesses could have been examined by the defence counsel, the defendant could have called witnesses who could have been examined by the prosecution, and the court could have reached a judgement based on full evidence. The inquisitor, by contrast, had no real evidence on which to reach a judgement except for the deposition of the accused man. A surprisingly large number of inquisitors wrote manuals for the guidance of their colleagues, and this may reflect the difficulties which they experienced in their work. Such a manual could be very useful: it could list the beliefs peculiar to different kinds of heretics and the questions which were appropriate to each sect; and it could warn against the subterfuges which members of particular sects employed and suggest ways of circumventing them. Yet despite these ancillary aids, an inquisitor must very often have based his decision on what we should term judgement of character, but what he would have called discernment of souls. This was an inevitable consequence of the strange way in which law enforcement and spiritual direction were closely associated in the work of this unique court.

5
Punishment and penance

The inquisitors were not empowered to pass sentence on offenders because they had no legal training. They had to take the advice of professional lawyers and of members of their own orders. Except for a brief period in the second half of the thirteenth century the concurrence of the diocesan bishop was also required before sentence could be passed. Some bishops regarded this as a formality and gave the inquisitors mandates to act on their behalf, but others insisted on being present. Such a body of judges could not be in permanent session, and normally it only met when the inquisitors had concluded their work in a particular area and there were a number of cases to be decided. Probably the opinions of experienced inquisitors normally carried great weight with the other assessors, but the final sentences were decided by the whole assembly and this process of consultation acted as a check on the arbitrary exercise of power by the Inquisition.

At any stage before judgement was given it was possible for an accused person to appeal directly to the pope. This happened comparatively rarely, presumably because such an appeal required a greater degree of sophistication, and also a great deal more money, than most suspects possessed. People who had the courage to appeal were often acquitted in the papal courts, perhaps because their readiness to submit to the pope's judgement was considered in itself strong presumptive evidence of their innocence. Once the Inquisition had pronounced sentence, however, there was no appeal from the judgement of the court.

Offenders who had confessed their guilt but refused to recant were normally handed over to the secular arm to be punished in accordance with the laws of the state: at this point they ceased to be under the Inquisition's jurisdiction. All other offenders who had confessed their guilt and retracted their errors remained in the tribunal's charge. The sentences which they received were not technically punishments, but penances. A punishment and a penance may look alike, but their purposes are quite distinct.

The doctrine of penance
All readers will be familiar with the concept of punishing offenders

49

who break the law, but since some may be less well informed about
the medieval doctrine of penance some explanation of it seems in
order here. This doctrine was formulated in precise and legalistic
terms which are alien to most modern kinds of religious thought.
It may therefore be helpful to bear in mind that the medieval
Catholic doctrine of penance and most traditional Protestant
teaching about the nature of the Atonement are based on an identical interpretation of God's justice.

Medieval theologians taught that grave, or mortal, sins cut the
soul off from God and, unless forgiven, would lead to damnation. A
penitent might be forgiven if he was truly contrite for his sin, if he
confessed it to a priest and received absolution, and if he performed the penance which the priest enjoined on him. Contrition
and absolution freed the sinner from the guilt and damnation
which his sin had incurred, by enabling him to share in the effects
of Christ's atoning sacrifice. God's justice, nevertheless, demanded
that the sinner should himself be punished for his sin, a process
which the theologians described as giving temporal satisfaction to
God. Penance was intended to meet this requirement either fully
or in part, and any temporal satisfaction which remained uncom-
pleted at death would have to be performed in purgatory. Penances only satisfied God's justice if they were undertaken willingly by the penitent as an expression of his contrition. The
Church had no means of enforcing the performance of penances
except by debarring from the sacraments any penitent who failed
to complete them.

In modern Catholic practice a canonical penance usually con-
sists in some private act of prayer. This convention has grown up
since the Counter-Reformation, but throughout the Middle Ages
the penances awarded for mortal sins remained harsh and were
often public. Thus the knights who murdered Thomas Becket were
required to go on pilgrimage to the Black Mountain of Antioch,
while Henry II was flogged by the monks of Christchurch, Canterbury, for his part in the murder.

The penances imposed by the Inquisition were, in many cases,
no harsher than those enjoined in sacramental confession at that
time. Heresy was regarded as a very grave sin which merited
severe penance. Inquisition penances differed from other penances in that they were enforced by legal sanctions. A man who
refused to accept an Inquisition penance would be handed over
to the secular arm as an impenitent heretic; a man who refused to
complete such a penance was liable to prosecution as a relapsed
heretic. Since the Church taught that a penance only had religious
value if it was performed willingly, it seems doubtful whether
the penalties which the Inquisition imposed on offenders were

really penances at all.

Yet the Inquisition had to use this vocabulary because it had no authority to punish offenders: that was the responsibility of the secular powers. The laws of most states in which the Inquisition operated decreed that heresy was punishable by death, and the abetting of heresy, whatever form it took, by the confiscation of property. If the inquisitors had been concerned simply with the extirpation of heresy they could have established the guilt of their suspects, handed them over to the secular arm and let the law take its course.

But they were also concerned to convert heretics and if a guilty man recanted they were unwilling to hand him over to the secular authorities to be punished for a past offence which he had repented. In this regard they were very lenient. A man found guilty of rape, for example, which was a capital offence in many medieval states, could not claim immunity from punishment because he had subsequently undergone a change of heart.

The inquisitors nevertheless faced a difficulty. If they protected repentant heretics from the rigours of the secular law and then merely exhorted them to make their confession to a priest in accordance with traditional Catholic practice, the heresy laws would be ineffective. In such a case there would have been every incentive for a heretic to tell the court that he repented, but there would have been no way of preventing him from resuming the practice of heresy after he had been released. The Inquisition would thus have failed in its main purpose, which was to check the spread of heresy; and would have become a kind of humane mouse-trap, from which all the mice were released at the end of each day with a solemn exhortation not to raid the larder again.

In their desire to temper law enforcement with mercy the inquisitors devised a compromise: this consisted in sentencing the penitent to a harsh penance which was legally enforceable. They succeeded in making the heresy laws respected in this way, but they brought the penitential system of the Church into disrepute.

Although the Inquisition heard cases in private, it pronounced judgement in public at the *Sermo Generalis*. This, as its name suggests, was a religious service. The people of the parish were assembled in church, together with all the suspects whom the inquisitor had examined. After preaching a homily the inquisitor read out the sentences, beginning with the least severe. These were canonical penances, which ranged from fasting on certain pre-scribed days, or additional church attendance, to public scourging (which was a penance, not a punishment), and pilgrimage. The shrines which had to be visited by those prescribed the penance of pilgrimage varied in number and distance: light penances only

involved visits to local shrines, whereas those guilty of serious
offences might be required to make pilgrimages to all the four
great shrines of western Europe, Rome, Compostella, Cologne and
Canterbury. In some cases a penitent was ordered to go to the
Holy Land, either as a pilgrim, or, if he was a knight, to serve for a
given number of years in the defence of the Crusader States. These
penances did not differ at all in kind from those which might have
been imposed in sacramental confession for a grave sin. Moreover,
the Inquisition was not unreasonable about enforcing such
penances. People who, on account of age or infirmity, were unable
to perform the penances enjoined on them, were given permission
either to commute them by giving alms for some charitable
purpose, or to find substitutes who were willing to carry out the
penances on their behalf.

The inquisitors devised a new form of penance, that of wearing
large yellow crosses on the clothing. This became the most
common of all Inquisition penances and superficially it appears a
very light one. It involved no physical hardship, it took up no time,
and the penitent could carry on with his normal life in the usual
way. Yet it was greatly feared, for, as the Jews discovered in
fascist states during the Second World War, wearing distinguish-
ing badges can cause great suffering in a repressive society. Penitents sentenced to crosses complained that they found difficulty in
obtaining work, that their neighbours ostracized them, and that
their children's marriage prospects were diminished, because
people were afraid of associating with those whom the Inquisition
had defamed as former heretics.

Imprisonment of offenders

More serious offenders were sentenced to imprisonment. Nowadays this is the most common form of punishment for criminal
offences, but the Inquisition was the first court to award this
penalty on a large scale. Previously crimes in western Europe
had normally been punished by the exaction of fines, by mutilation, or by death. Special prisons had to be built for the use of
the Inquisition, and it was often a matter of dispute whether the
cost should be borne by the secular authorities or the bishop.
These prisons came under the jurisdiction of the Inquisition and
only the pope had the right to supervise them, which he rarely
exercised.

There were two types of Inquisition prison: the *murus largus,* or
broad wall, and the *murus strictus,* or narrow wall. Both consisted
of blocks of cells. The *murus largus* seems to have been modelled
on a monastery. Prisoners were detained there in separate cells,

which had windows to admit light and air; they were not chained, and were allowed into the yard from time to time for exercise and thus enjoyed some measure of social intercourse with each other. Suspects awaiting sentence were held in the *murus largus,* together with prisoners whose offence was not too grave. The *murus strictus* was a maximum security prison: it was modelled on dungeons, which it closely resembled. The cells normally had no windows, and prisoners were chained, sometimes to the walls, and had no exercise at all. The diet of all Inquisition prisoners was spartan, consisting of bread and water only. Prisoners were not allowed to receive visits, except for married people who might be regularly visited by their wives or husbands.

The prisons were run by lay staff whom the Inquisition employed. They could be bribed, and the harsh conditions of prison life could be mitigated with their connivance. Gifts of food and clothing could reach prisoners in this way, and so could unauthorized visitors. On occasion even a Cathar *perfectus* might be smuggled into a prison to console a believer, and the bravery of such men commands admiration because they risked death by burning if they were detected. It is clear from the frequency with which papal complaints on the subject were made that the strict rules governing the life of Inquisition prisons were regularly circumvented.

When they were sentenced offenders were ordered to report to prison, there to do penance on a diet of bread and water. Their attendance had to be voluntary, otherwise it would not have qualified as a penance, but failure to comply with the injunction was treated as a relapse into heresy, meriting more severe measures. Prison sentences were officially given for life, although the practice was more flexible than this.

Imprisonment differed from the other canonical penances imposed by the Inquisition in that it had never been used as a penance in sacramental confession. It was not, however, a complete innovation in penitential practice. In the ascetic tradition of the Church self-inflicted penance had for centuries held an honoured place as a means of sharing in the sufferings of Christ and thus in His redemptive work. All over Europe in the later Middle Ages anchorites of both sexes lived in cells which they never left, like the fourteenth-century English mystic Lady Julian of Norwich. Their conditions of life were not outwardly very different from those of the prisoners of the *murus largus.* A few ascetics, indeed, had from time to time embraced a life not unlike that of the prisoners of the *murus strictus* and had been praised for their outstanding holiness: the stylite saints are examples of this. In that sense the penances which the Inquisition imposed on their prisoners had a respectable pedigree.

But the comparison ended there. Anchorites and ascetics deliberately chose to perform penances of this kind: they were not obliged to enter upon them and they were liable to no secular penalty if they abandoned them. A stylite who came down from his pillar was not committing an indictable offence. The prisoners of the Inquisition had no free choice: they were guilty of a criminal offence if they refused to accept or to complete the penance assigned to them. Moreover, the penances were unsuited to men and women who had received no training in the contemplative life. The chief burden of imprisonment in the *murus largus* must have been lack of occupation: detainees were given no work and, unlike anchorites, they had received no training in the life of prayer. The prisoners of the *murus strictus* were deprived of almost all the concomitants of human dignity: it may be meritorious to choose to suffer in this way as part of the imitation of Christ, but it must be very difficult indeed to accept such suffering in the right spirit if it is forced upon you.

The inquisitors' problem was a real one. They imprisoned men whom they suspected would relapse into heresy if they were released, thereby frustrating the work of the tribunal. Because these offenders had recanted, the Inquisition was unwilling to hand them over to the secular arm, even though they doubted their sincerity. Common prudence suggested that they should be imprisoned, but as the Inquisition only had authority to inflict spiritual penalties they had to call this punishment a penance. It was another instance of the difficulties which inquisitors encountered when they tried to discharge two incompatible functions simultaneously: those of law enforcement and spiritual direction.

The state sometimes confiscated the property of inquisition prisoners, as the legislation of Lucius III and Innocent III empowered it to do, but this was not invariable. This was a secular punishment and did not form part of the Inquisition's sentence, nor did the tribunal recommend it. The only part of a heretic's property which was immune from confisation was his wife's dowry if she was a good Catholic. Innocent IV was responsible for introducing this exemption, which was necessary, because a woman who was simultaneously deprived of her husband's earning power and all her property was left completely destitute.

Handing over to the secular arm

Offenders who had admitted to being heretics, but who had refused to recant, were handed over to the secular arm. When pronouncing this sentence the inquisitor usually made a formal recommendation for mercy. Most modern commentators have regarded this as a sickening piece of hypocrisy, but such criticism is misdirected. The inquisitors were totally indifferent to public opinion, and had no wish to be thought of as kindly men who disliked capital punishment; nor can they have supposed that their statement would be taken at its face-value by God. Their intention was to safeguard themselves against any charge of canonical irregularity which they might incur if, as priests, they tacitly agreed to a judgement of blood.

The secular authorities normally burned the condemned men in some public place, in accordance with the laws of the state, immediately the *Sermo Generalis* had ended. The property of those condemned to death was always confiscated by the secular rulers, but since in the thirteenth century the vast majority of those who were burnt were perfected Cathars, vowed to total poverty, this cannot have proved a very fruitful source of revenue.

The *Sermo Generalis* concluded with the sentencing of dead heretics. Their bones were then disinterred and publicly burnt. Public sensibility was deeply shocked by this, for in the Middle Ages the bodies of the dead were customarily treated with a reverence which was still largely pagan in many of its manifestations. The Inquisition intended these macabre *autos-da-fé* to be outrageous, since it wished to demonstrate that unrepentant heretics had no place in a Christian society, and that even after their death they polluted graveyards by their presence.

The heirs of a dead heretic also suffered, since his property was liable to confiscation by the secular authorities even if his heirs were of unimpeachable orthodoxy. Moreover, his heirs were debarred from holding public office for two generations, although Pope Boniface VIII later exempted descendants in the female line from this penalty.

The names of some suspects were not read out at the *Sermo Generalis*: these were people who were being held for further questioning. They could be detained indefinitely at the Inquisition's pleasure, and were usually held in the *murus largus*. There were a variety of reasons which might lead to such a situation: a Cathar believer, for example, might not wish to compromise his convictions by recanting, yet might not be prepared to die for his beliefs. For the Cathars had no doctrine of baptism by desire: an unconsoled believer, even if he died for the faith, would be re-incarnated, and thus such a man had every incentive to stay alive. Other men might be detained because they refused to denounce their friends or kindred; while some might refuse to recant because they wished to protect their dependants from want, since the property of a man who had not been sentenced could not be confiscated, however long he remained in prison.

The inquisitors developed the system of cross-referencing their records. This seems to have been previously unknown, although it is now a standard part of all administrative practice. Consequently any offender who was brought before the tribunal a second time could be identified, however long ago his first offence had been committed. This happened chiefly in the case of people who had been given canonical penances and had subsequently reverted to heresy. Such offenders were known as relapsed heretics, as were those who refused to complete the penances which had been enjoined upon them. Those who escaped from the prisons of the Inquisition were included in the second category. The legal penalty for relapsing into heresy was death at the stake, but this was almost never invoked. Such people usually recanted a second time and were treated as penitents, but their penance for a second offence was more severe. They were usually imprisoned, and if their second offence was gaol-breaking they might be condemned to the *murus strictus* from which escape was almost impossible.

In theory it should not have been difficult to escape from the Inquisition. There were large areas of Europe in which it did not operate, and movement between states was far easier in the Middle Ages than it is now, for there were then no passports and no frontier posts. Yet most people at the time were not at all cosmopolitan in outlook: their imaginative horizons were bounded by the familiar area in which they had grown up. Many people who tried to escape from the Inquisition went into hiding in their own villages, or became outlaws in the wilder parts of their own regions, and they were easily recaptured. The one group of people who successfully evaded capture were young men without family ties who were willing to serve as mercenaries, for they could find employment in any part of the Christian world, and could go to places like Frankish Greece where the Inquisition did not operate.

Only the pope could grant complete pardon from penances enjoined by the Inquisition, and he sometimes did so. Thus Innocent IV granted an indulgence to all prisoners of the Inquisition in Languedoc who were willing to take part in St Louis's crusade. An inquisitor, however, had the discretion to decide when a penance had been satisfactorily completed. Bernard Gui, for example, during his 17 years as inquisitor of Toulouse, released 87 people from wearing crosses and 119 from prison sentences. A prisoner whose property had been confiscated would certainly receive at least part of it back if he obtained a papal pardon, and might be similarly treated if the inquisitor released him from his penance.

In one way the Inquisition achieved what it set out to do. It substituted the rule of law for mob violence in the prosecution of heresy. Contrary to popular belief the inquisitors handed very few people over to the secular arm to be burnt at the stake. Bernard of Caux, for example, sentenced 207 offenders between 12 May and 22 July 1246, when prosecutions for heresy were at their height in Languedoc: none of those convicted was burnt and only 23 were imprisoned, the remaining 184 were condemned to wear crosses. This is not an exceptional sample: in the period 1249–57 the papal and episcopal inquisitions in southern France between them sentenced 230 people to imprisonment, but only handed 21 offenders over to the secular arm. Thus less than three people a year were burned on average in Languedoc when the campaign against heresy there was fiercest. Once the Inquisition was established, except for isolated instances which will be considered later in this work, the pyromania which had characterized lay attempts to suppress heresy came to an end.

Effectiveness of the Inquisition

It is more difficult to know how effective the Inquisition was in checking the spread of heresy. People who were Catholics at heart, but who had shown some sympathy for Cathars, were probably frightened into strict orthodoxy by the activities of the Inquisition. People who had previously had no association with Catharism were less likely to become involved with it once persecution had started. To that extent the Inquisition probably made it more difficult for the Cathars to proselytize, but such conclusions can only be tentative, because persecution can have the opposite effect and give publicity to dissenting minorities.

Catharism certainly died out all over western Europe within 90 years of the setting up of the Inquisition, although it survived longer in Bosnia. It is tempting to see this as a straightforward process of cause and effect, but such a simplistic view is open to the criticism that persecution normally results in the wider diffusion of a movement. Catharism had simultaneously to face other kinds of opposition: the pastoral work of the friars on the one hand, which has already been described in chapter three; and on the other the criticism of Catholic intellectuals, which certainly led some Cathar theologians, like the author of *The Book of the Two Principles,* to take up a position nearer to that of the Catholic Church, and which must have weakened the appeal of Catharism as a radical, alternative religious system. Yet in some ways Catharism was more vulnerable to persecution than most religions are. The church consisted solely of the perfect, who needed rigorous training to enable them to live the unusually austere life that their profession entailed. Such training necessitated the existence of houses of study, and provision could not be made for these once persecution became at all general. When the perfect could no longer be trained the religion was doomed, since they alone could confer the sacrament of salvation. It is, however, arguable that a more vital leadership would have sought to establish Cathar centres of study in places where the Inquisition did not operate, which were numerous, and that the Cathars' failure to do so indicates that the movement had already begun to lose its vigour when the persecution started. Nevertheless, it is fair to assume that although the Inquisition may not have been solely, or even chiefly, responsible for the collapse of Catharism, it accelerated that process.

Equally impossible to quantify is the extent to which the Inquisition succeeded in converting heretics to the true faith. In the case of the Cathar *perfecti* their success rate was negligible: these men and women died with dignity in the faith which they believed to be true. Believers, who lacked the assurance of salvation which the *consolamentum* alone could give them, were usually willing to recant and to conform outwardly to the Catholic cult. It is impossible to tell how far they gave inward assent to orthodox beliefs, but it seems unlikely that they held in any great esteem a Church which coerced them into performing penance and which was willing, on occasion, to torture and imprison them in its zeal to save their souls.

The Inquisition was founded to detect heresy, and it discharged that task with great efficiency. Its work was clearly beneficial in so far as it replaced mob violence by the rule of law. Moreover, contrary to popular opinion, it was surprisingly lenient in its treatment of offenders: 90 per cent of its sentences were canonical penances; only a small minority of those whom it convicted were put in prison; while the number who were put to death was very small indeed.

Nevertheless, the Inquisition was viewed with detestation by much contemporary opinion, and justly so, because it tried to coerce people into right belief. Queen Elizabeth I of England, when faced with a problem of widespread religious disaffection not dissimilar from that which faced the Inquisition, showed a better understanding of the limitations of coercion in matters of religion. Her penal laws enforced outward conformity with the established church on all her subjects and forbade the practice of any other public cult, but she refused to legislate about her subjects' beliefs, declaring that she would not open windows into any man's soul.

Such realism implies detachment, and this is a quality which it is, perhaps, unreasonable to look for in the Inquisition, which strove to extirpate heresy not because it imperilled the public peace, but because it endangered men's souls. Nevertheless, by opening windows into those souls the inquisitors aroused hatred, their clemency was forgotten, and they brought the Church which they served into disrepute.

6
The Inquisition in Languedoc 1233—1324

The last two chapters may have given the impression that the Inquisition was from its inception a monolithic institution, which was assured of success if it had the support of lay rulers. This was far from being the case. Initially inquisitors were appointed in particular areas and were granted special powers by the pope to enforce the Church's heresy laws; but they had to devise effective methods of working; they met with considerable opposition from the heretics themselves; and, not infrequently, they antagonized some of their own potential supporters. In order to survive the Inquisition had to overcome these problems, to develop an effective form of procedure and organization, and to prove its value not only to the Church, but to the state as well.

This process can be observed most clearly in the case of the Inquisition in Languedoc (that part of southern France in which 'oc' was used instead of the northern French 'oeil' to mean 'yes'). The tribunal had a greater chance of achieving success there than anywhere else in western Europe. As a result of the Albigensian crusades much of the eastern part of this region had been annexed by the French crown, and although Count Raymond VII of Toulouse had retained some measure of independence in his ancestral lands, he could not afford to provoke another war with the king of France by refusing to co-operate with the Church. During the formative years of the Inquisition in Languedoc France was ruled first by the regent, Blanche of Castile, and then by her son, St Louis, both of whom were prepared to co-operate fully with the holy see in its efforts to stamp out heresy. Moreover, when the Inquisition was first set up there it could expect the support of the southern French bishops, most of whom had been nominated in the course of the Albigensian crusades because of their zeal in the cause of orthodoxy. Yet despite all these favourable circumstances, the Inquisition in Languedoc was very insecure for almost 40 years after its foundation.

It was formally inaugurated in 1233 when Pope Gregory IX ordered the Dominican provincial of Toulouse to appoint members of his order, learned in theology, to make inquisition for heresy in the provinces of Narbonne, Bourges, Auch and Bordeaux. Their primary function was to prosecute Cathars, but, of course, any other kind of heresy was within the competence of their tribunal. Consequently some Waldensians were brought to trial, but as long as Catharism remained vigorous the inquisitors were not centrally interested in persecuting the Waldensian church, which remained close to that of Rome in its faith and practice.

The inquisitors began their work in 1234. Catharism was still widely diffused throughout the whole area and among all classes: the mass burnings which had taken place during the Albigensian crusades had not diminished the vigour of the movement. But, since the region had, directly or indirectly, come under royal rule, and attempts had been made to enforce the heresy laws, Catharism was no longer practised openly in most places. Cathar believers had always been indistinguishable from Catholic laymen, but the perfect had also adopted lay dress by the time the Inquisition was founded, and had closed down their houses and dispersed their members among the households of lay sympathizers. The inquisitors therefore had some difficulty in knowing where to begin their work.

In a situation of this kind, where people with heretical sympathies formed a sizable part of the population, any prosecution which the inquisitors initiated was bound to appear arbitrary and to cause resentment. That this was what happened is clear from the account of William Pelhisson, one of the first inquisitors in Languedoc. He tells how, when Friar Arnold Catalan began his work of inquisition at Albi, he secured the arrest and condemnation of two *perfecti*, but that when he sentenced a dead *perfecta* the civil authorities refused to disinter the body, and when he tried to do so himself he was almost beaten to death by an infuriated mob.

At this time the inquisitors had not been working for long enough to be distinguished in the public mind from the rest of their order. The bishop of Toulouse, Raymond of Miramont, was himself a Dominican, and in the long term this was of great help to the Inquisition because he co-operated fully in their work. Nevertheless, it was initially something of a handicap, because he was zealous in his desire to aid them in the suppression of heresy, but was not subject to their authority or bound to observe their procedures. An example of the problems this created occurred in 1234, when news of St Dominic's canonization reached Toulouse and the bishop went to celebrate Mass in the house of the Friars Preacher. News was brought to him that an elderly woman, who was dangerously ill, had been hereticated in a nearby house, and he went to call on her. Her household had no opportunity to warn her who he was, and she seems to have supposed that he was the

Cathar bishop, for she freely confessed her faith to him. He then adjured her to recant, and, when she refused, summoned the count's representative, who ordered her to be carried out of the city in her bed and publicly burnt. The inquisitors fully sympathized with this decision, but it was not the work of their tribunal and the bishop had not used their methods. So far as I am aware the Inquisition itself never perpetrated a parallel outrage in the medieval centuries, yet in the minds of the people of Toulouse this act must have been associated with the inquisitors, who were present at the burning. It can have done nothing to re-assure public opinion that the new tribunal was intent on converting heretics rather than convicting them, and of giving them, by its own standards, a fair trial.

Inevitably the Inquisition met with strong opposition when it tried to attack the powerful. Some of the consular families of Toulouse were Cathar supporters, but the inquisitors who cited them for heresy were expelled from the city, and so, soon afterwards, was the entire Dominican convent, together with the bishop. The Inquisition of Toulouse then became a bargaining counter in a complicated game of international politics. Pope Gregory IX could not afford to ignore the way in which the inquisitors had been treated, because they were his representatives. He therefore reminded the count of Toulouse that he had not yet fulfilled the crusader vow which had been part of the price he had agreed to pay to end the war with France in 1229. Since the count wished neither to go to the Holy Land nor to be excommunicated, he used his influence to persuade the consuls of Toulouse to readmit the Dominicans and, with them, the inquisitors. But the burgesses of Touolse had been loyal allies of the count's in the wars of the Albigensian crusade, and he had no intention of sacrificing them to the fanaticism of the Church. He therefore lodged a complaint with the pope that the inquisitors bore him mortal enmity, and while this charge was being investigated they could take no action against the consuls, who were theoretically his officials. At this point, the pope, who was at war with the Emperor Frederick II, feared that the count of Toulouse might ally with the emperor if provoked, and in 1238 he therefore suspended the inquisitors of Toulouse. Their power was only restored in 1241, and even then they were only allowed to operate outside Toulouse city.

This illustrates the kind of problems which the inquisitors faced in their early years. If they ordered the arrest of perfected Cathars they were likely to be obeyed by the secular authorities who did not want to run the risk of offending the pope and incurring excommunication in such clear-cut cases. But this happened comparatively rarely because the perfect were skilful in evading capture. If the inquisitors ordered the arrest of poor believers, they could usually count on the help of the civil authorities, but this did not strike at the heart of Catharism, because such people did not have the facilities to shelter the perfect and organize clandestine religious meetings. If, on the other hand, the inquisitors moved against powerful believers, who had such facilities, they were likely to become involved in political issues, and the decisions which were finally made in such cases were often not determined on grounds of orthodoxy at all. For, as the case of the consuls of Toulouse showed, the pope himself was not necessarily willing to support the inquisitors in their fight against heresy in all circumstances.

The fortress of Montségur

The weakness of the Inquisition's power at this time may be gauged from the fact that 10 years after its inception the Cathar bishops of Toulouse and Agen lived openly in the castle of Montségur. This fortress has attracted as much ill founded speculation as the Grail castle of Corbenic, with which at least one writer has identified it. It seems extremely unlikely that it held any religious significance for the Cathars, who regarded shrines, and all material symbols, with contempt, but it undoubtedly was of great practical value to them. Its lord, Raymond of Perelha, was a Cathar believer. The bishops could peacefully direct the affairs of their churches from his castle; postulants could receive there the strict and lengthy training which the novitiate demanded; and the perfect who were not engaged in the work of public ministry could lead the contemplative life there. This was public knowledge throughout Languedoc, and the most sensible way of attacking, Catharism there would have been to suppress Montségur. This would have presented no political difficulty, since the lordship was part of the territory directly ruled by the French crown. Yet no attempt was made to arrest Raymond of Perelha, the most notorious defender of heretics in southern France, or to convict the numerous *perfecti* who lived there. The reason for this lack of action was a practical one. Montségur was a very difficult castle to besiege: any attempt to do so would tie up a large number of troops for a long time and be very expensive. It was not a rich lordship and the financial reward that its capture would afford was negligible, and the secular authorities were not willing to go to such lengths to aid the Inquisition in the suppression of heresy.

The castle finally fell because attention was drawn to it by the action of its military commander, Roger of Mirepoix, who, in

1242, with the help of other members of the garrison, attacked and killed William Arnaud, inquisitor of Toulouse, together with his companions, while they were staying in the town of Avignonet. From the garrison's point of view this must have seemed a sensible policy: the work of inquisition had only just been resumed after a break of three years, and it may well have seemed possible that the murder of the inquisitors would cause the experiment to be discontinued.

In retrospect it is evident that this was a serious miscalculation. The inquisitors were the pope's representatives, and the holy see could not ignore their assassination. The Avignonet incident was not very different in character from the murder of the pope's legate which had sparked off the Albigensian crusades in 1208. The lord of Montségur had no powerful protectors who could use their influence to block retaliatory measures. Accordingly the seneschal of Carcassonne mustered an army in 1243 and attacked the castle, which fell after 10 months' siege in 1244. The believers present were told to report at a later date to the Inquisition, but the perfect were given no choice. The were offered the alternative of death or recantation; all of them chose death; and on the day that the castle was surrendered 215 *perfecti* were burnt at the foot of the mountain in one great fire. The Inquisition had no part in this mass execution, which was organized by the secular authorities.

The count of Toulouse and the royal officials, who between them ruled Languedoc in the king's name, were anxious to placate the papacy by showing their zeal for orthodoxy. As a result, the new inquisitors of Toulouse, John of St Pierre and Bernard of Caux, were able to conduct their investigations in the years following the fall of Montségur on a scale which would have been unthinkable to their predecessors. Whole villages were called in for questioning. Yet at this point, when the Inquisition seemed to have finally established itself in Languedoc, its position was undermined from an unexpected quarter.

Papal intervention

Pope Innocent IV had fled from Rome late in 1244 to escape from the Emperor Frederick, and came to Lyons, to which he had summoned a general council of the Church, which met in 1245. The pope stayed there until after Frederick's death in 1250. It might have been supposed that the pope's presence would strengthen the power of the Inquisition, but, as Dossat has shown in *Les Crises de l' Inquisition toulousaine au XIIIe siècle*, it had the opposite effect. In the first place it was much easier for people to appeal to the pope from the Inquisition when he was living in Languedoc than when he was in Rome: 156 inhabitants of Limoux made a successful appeal of this kind in 1246. Secondly, the pope could supervise the work of inquisition more closely when he was in southern France himself. He first offered an indulgence to prisoners of the Inquisition who were willing to serve on St Louis's crusade, and then in 1249 sent his penitentiary to the dioceses of Agen, Cahors, Rodez, Albi and Toulouse with powers to commute any Inquisition sentence.

Papal intervention on this scale undermined the authority of the inquisitors. Moreover, their orders did not like supplying brethren for that work, less, it would seem, because they found the prosecution of heresy uncongenial, than because friars who served as inquisitors were in effect exempt from the authority of their religious superiors. In 1249, therefore, the mendicants of Languedoc withdrew completely from the work of inquisition. This was resumed by the bishops, who had performed this duty before 1233. The work of lay prosecution of heresy also continued, and in 1249 Raymond VII ordered his officials to burn 80 relapsed Cathar believers at Agen. This was the last large-scale burning to take place in Languedoc.

Episcopal tribunals were not as efficient as the Inquisition in seeking out heretics. This is clear from the situation in Narbonne. The archbishop excluded the Inquisition from the city in 1237 and, as Emery has shown, between that date and 1318 when it began to operate there again, there were only 10 known instances of prosecutions for heresy at Narbonne, almost all of Waldensians. This would seem to prove the point that bishops were busy men who could only devote a limited time to the prosecution of heretics. That work could only be effectively carried out by full-time inquisitors. This was certainly the opinion of Innocent IV's successor, Alexander IV, who reconstituted the Inquisition in Languedoc in 1255 with greater powers than it had previously possessed. The inquisitors were freed from any kind of obedience to their own religious superiors and were even released from the authority of papal legates. Moreover, they were also relieved from the obligation to obtain the assent of the diocesan bishop to any sentence they gave, although that privilege was later rescinded by Pope Gregory X (1272—6).

Yet when they resumed work again the inquisitors were faced by a quite different situation from that which had confronted their predecessors. The fall of Montségur had been a blow to the organization of part of the Cathar church in Languedoc, but the death of Raymond VII of Toulouse in 1249 was an even more serious setback for Catharism. Although the count had not been personally well-disposed towards heresy, he had employed southern

French officials, who had grown up in a society where Catharism was deeply rooted, and who were prepared to ignore the activities of Cathars in their area. Raymond was succeeded by his son-in-law, Alphonse of Poitiers, younger brother of St Louis, who employed northern French officials in the lands of Toulouse, and they were not prepared to connive at the presence of Cathars there. Thus throughout Languedoc after 1249 the secular and ecclesiastical authorities were united in their desire to enforce the heresy laws.

Moreover, the earlier persecution, by the papal Inquisition, by bishops and by lay officials, although it had been eclectic, had not been without effect. The great nobility and the rich bourgeoisie became afraid of associating with heretics, because this could lead to imprisonment and the confiscation of property. St Louis had undermined support for the Cathars among the nobility even more by restoring lands to those among them who had been convicted of heresy but who had availed themselves of Innocent IV's indulgence and had served him loyally on his crusade. Such families recognized that they would only be able to retain their restored estates if they preserved an unblemished reputation for orthodoxy.

As a result of the loss of powerful patrons, the Cathars lacked secure places of refuge in Languedoc which would serve them as headquarters and as training centres for postulants. From about 1250 the hierarchy and the majority of the perfect began to withdraw to Lombardy where, for reasons which will be discussed in the next chapter, the heresy laws were not uniformly enforced. This was not a sudden exodus, but a gradual process extending over many years. It began in about 1250, but Peter Polanh, Cathar bishop of Carcassonne, remained in southern France, for example, until his death in c.1267. The erosion of support for the Cathars among the rich and powerful was equally gradual, and there remained some families who were willing to risk the heavy penalties which attached to sheltering the perfect.

But by about 1270 the character of southern French Catharism had changed. The hierarchy lived in Lombardy and established training centres there for postulants and houses for *perfecti* who were not engaged in public ministry. They were visited by believers from Languedoc, who wanted counsel and instruction, and they sent a number of *perfecti* to southern France to work among believers.

The perfect who continued to operate in Languedoc were constantly on the move, living in woods and caves, and holding meetings by night, often in the open air. They entered towns and villages only when summoned to console dying believers. In such circumstances it was essential to set up a network of agents, who knew who the believers were and also where the perfect were to be found, and who could put one group in touch with the other. Such agents were paid well by the Cathar church: it was dangerous work, since they risked life imprisonment if they were caught.

The inquisitors' new problems

The inquisitors thus had to deal with a secret society. In one way this made their work much easier, since all they needed to do was to concentrate on capturing the few *perfecti* and their more numerous agents. If they could break the network which linked the Cathars of Languedoc with the Italian headquarters of the movement they would be within sight of success, because they would then have to deal only with leaderless believers, who could no longer be contaminated by fresh heretical contacts. Had they confined themselves to this work they would probably have met with little opposition, except perhaps from believers, who were declining in numbers.

Quite the opposite happened. The Inquisition became unpopular with a wide section of the population, few of whom were any longer actively involved with Catharism. This resulted from the economic problems which the Inquisition faced. The estates of heretics condemned to death or to imprisonment were liable to confiscation by the secular authorities, and in the early days of persecution, when heresy was widespread, large amounts of property had accrued in this way to the French crown and the counts of Toulouse. Confiscations were not always as profitable as might be supposed. The dower rights of Catholic wives of convicted heretics were protected by canon law, but the rights of Catholic creditors of condemned heretics were protected by civil law, and few of the confiscated estates were unencumbered with debts of some kind, which diminished their value. The lay authorities were required to meet the expenses of the inquisitors from the revenues of such properties. The inquisitors, who were vowed to poverty, did not receive salaries, but the members of their households did; the living expenses and the heavy travelling expenses of the inquisitors and their staffs had to be met; the buildings which they used as their headquarters had to be maintained, and so did the prisons of the Inquisition. The wages of the prison staff and the maintenance of the prisoners were likewise the responsibility of the secular authorities. As all modern taxpayers know, prison services are expensive, and lay rulers were appalled by the high costs of the Inquisition and complained to the popes about the extravagance of the tribunal. There seems, from surviving accounts of inquisitors' expenses, to have been little foundation in such allegations, but the running costs of the Inquisition were quite high. Nevertheless, in the early years the Inquisition cost the state nothing, and secular princes even made some profit from the confiscation of heretics' property, although less than might have been expected.

As heretics became fewer, and as the propertied classes withdrew their support from them, so the value of confiscations declined, while the expenses of the Inquisition remained constant. It seemed doubtful whether secular rulers would be prepared to pay for a service of this kind if it changed from being a source of marginal profit to being a major expense. The inquisitors found means of dealing with his problem. One method was to prosecute the dead. Inquisition records contained evidence about prosperous believers who had been hereticated on their deathbeds before the persecution began. The grandchildren of such men were liable under both canon and civil law to have their property confiscated if the inquisitors secured a conviction, and it was difficult to prevent them from doing so, since, with the passage of time, few witnesses remained alive who could contest the truth of their accusations. This kind of prosecution obviously caused resentment among the victims, who were often good Catholics, and who in some cases could not remember the time when their families had had Cathar sympathies. The longest known span of time between an heretication and a prosecution is 70 years. This was a terminal problem, since the property of heirs in the third generation was not liable to confiscation. Another method which the inquisitors sometimes used was to give prison sentences for minor offences, since such awards were followed by confiscation. Thus, as G.W.Davis has shown in *The Inquisition at Albi, 1299-1300,* the 25 leading citizens of Albi imprisoned by the Inquisition for heresy in 1299 probably had been guilty of associating with Cathar *perfecti,* but their degree of involvement would, at an earlier period, only have attracted canonical penances.

Although the mass of the population do not seem to have objected to the lawful exercise of inquisitorial power in the tracking down of genuine heretics, there was general opposition to what were rightly seen as acts of oppression, engineered to justify the seizure of property. The inquisitors were widely criticized, and sometimes physically assaulted, and, when attempts at intimidation failed to produce results, the cities of Languedoc appealed for help to the king of France. He was St Louis's grandson, Philip IV, who, though no more disposed to tolerate heresy than his predecessors, was attempting to centralize authority throughout his kingdom, and was therefore anxious to reduce the powers of exempt jurisdictions, of which that of the Inquisition was an outstanding example. In 1291 he instructed the seneschal of Carcassonne not to arrest anybody on the orders of the Inquisition unless he was notoriously defamed as a heretic. This did not abrogate the powers of the tribunal, but was effective in checking the abuse of them.

Philip's desire to bring the Inquisition more strictly under royal control did not vary, despite vacillations in this policy brought about by his need to make concessions to the holy see during his quarrel with Boniface VIII about the right of the pope to tax the French clergy. In 1304, after Boniface's death, King Philip appointed royal commissioners to inspect the Inquisition prisons, a right which had hitherto been reserved to the pope.

Clement V, who became pope in 1305 and was responsible for moving the seat of papal government to Avignon, where it remained until 1378, was equally anxious to reform the Inquisition, and was better placed to supervise its work in Languedoc than any pope since Innocent IV. In 1306 he appointed a legatine commission to inspect the Inquisition prisons and they were critical of the conditions they found. At Carcassonne they ordered new accommodation to be built for the 40 prisoners, and they dismissed the prison staff. It seemed possible that the Inquisition in Languedoc might lose much of its power, since both king and pope were concerned to restrict its autonomy. But in 1307 the Knights Templar were accused of heresy and the Inquisition was charged with the task of prosecuting them. This was clearly not an appropriate time to reduce the powers of the tribunal. Although the Council of Vienne in 1312 restricted the Inquisition's powers by enacting that the concurrence of the diocesan bishop must be sought before a suspect might be imprisoned or tortured, no major reforms were made. This canon caused procedural delays in the work of the Inquisition, but was only effective in cases where bishops were prepared to exercise supervisory powers, which not all of them were.

The decline of Catharism

It would appear that active Catharism had almost died out in Languedoc by 1290, partly because the headquarters of the Cathar church in Lombardy was simultaneously under attack, but the vacillating policy of the crown, and, indeed, of the papacy, towards the Inquisition in the next 16 years made a recrudescence of Catharism possible in Languedoc. This was largely the work of a single man, Peter Autier, a notary of Foix, who in 1295—6 went to Italy with his brother William, where they received a full training in Catharism and were consoled. In 1298 they returned to

Languedoc and spent the next 11 years in active ministry, chiefly in the county of Foix, but ranging as far afield as Cahors. Peter Autier found support in 125 places in Languedoc, and is reckoned by Vidal to have ministered to some 1,000 believers, although it is notable that they were almost all of them poor people, whereas at its height Catharism had attracted support from all social classes.

Catharism was not dead in Languedoc in the early fourteenth century, but it lacked powerful patrons or effective leadership. Yet the impact which one minister could make in the area justified the Inquisition in its belief that it must never relax its vigilance. Bernard Gui, who became inquisitor of Toulouse in 1307, spent most of his career in tracking down this last Cathar remnant. Peter Autier was captured in 1309 and went to his death two years later, saying to the crowd: 'If it were lawful for me to preach, you would all accept my faith'.

Despite his great gifts Peter Autier had not been able to train adequate successors. He had endeavoured to do so, and had consoled some *perfecti*, but his life, which was that of a perpetual fugitive, did not provide the necessary conditions of stability for giving a training to others in asceticism and theology such as he had received himself in the more peaceful conditions of Italy. This is apparent from the career of the *perfectus* William Belibaste, whom Autier had trained, and who subsequently led a group of believers to found a Cathar colony in Catalonia, where the inquisition of Toulouse could not reach them. Belibaste could not live the life of the perfect and had a very imperfect grasp of Cathar theology. He was a pathetic character, and in no sense a danger to the Church. But he did not escape the attention of Bernard Gui, and was lured within the jurisdiction of the inquisition of Toulouse, arrested, and burnt in 1321.

Thereafter there may have been Cathar believers in Languedoc: there may even have been some *perfecti*, but, if so, they were people who had been hereticated when dying and had subsequently recovered. Such people had received no formal instruction in the faith and, although technically empowered to confer the *consolamentum*, did not know how to do so. No more *perfecti* came from Italy, and although Cathar believers were detected for some years to come in Languedoc, by the time Bernard Gui retired as inquisitor of Toulouse in 1324 to become bishop of Lodève, southern French Catharism was dead.

As was said in the previous chapter, it is debatable whether the decline of Catharism should be attributed mainly to the work of the Inquisition. Yet people at the time undoubtedly thought that it should, and could point to the way in which heresy revived again immediately the vigilance of the inquisitors was relaxed. The fact that the Inquisition had succeeded in eradicating Catharism almost completely did not deprive it of its *raison d'être,* although it might have been expected to have done so. On the contrary, its conduct of the trial of the Templars had shown that it was flexible and could deal with all kinds of disorder in Christian society. Indeed, during the last stage of the Cathar persecution the papacy had already begun to use the Inquisition to deal with the Spiritual Franciscans, whom it regarded as a new threat to the peace of the Church. The Inquisition's dealings with the Templars and with the Spiritual Franciscans were not confined to Languedoc, and are best considered in a later chapter. But the Inquisition in Languedoc had in the first century of its existence overcome all its crises, and was recognized as an established part of society, with its own buildings, employees and exempt jurisdiction. It had proved its worth to the Church by its enforcement of orthodoxy, and to the state by its confiscation of property, and its right to exist was not subsequently challenged.

7
The growth of the Inquisition

The Inquisition was unique among the institutions of the medieval Western Church in that it did not become uniformly established in all parts of Catholic Christendom. This was, in part, a consequence of the specialist nature of its work. There was, for example, no need to establish the Inquisition in England, because there was virtually no heresy there to prosecute between c.1200 and the end of the fourteenth century. When Lollardy became widespread the English authorities reacted towards heretics in exactly the same way as the holy see, and the statute *De Haeretico Comburendo* of 1401 enacted that heretics who refused to recant should be burnt alive. Nevertheless, such cases were tried in the normal ecclesiastical courts and the Inquisition was not introduced. It was not established in the neighbouring kingdom of Scotland either, or in Scandinavia, because in all those states heresy was comparatively rare.

For rather different reasons the Inquisition was not introduced in areas where Latin Christians were in a minority. Rulers may have feared that inquisitors would cause civil unrest by prosecuting their eastern-rite Christian subjects for deviating from western norms of practice and belief. There were no inquisitors in Frankish Greece or Lusignan Cyprus. Pope Nicholas IV, it is true, ordered the Inquisition to be founded in the kingdom of Acre in 1290, but the Mamluk conquest of the remaining Frankish territory there in the following year made this injunction inoperative. The pope may have reached this decision in response to the special circumstances of Frankish Syria, for many penitent heretics were enjoined to go there on pilgrimage by the Inquisition in western Europe and this rendered the Crusader Kingdom particularly vulnerable to the spread of heterodoxy. The most unexpected instance of a state in which the medieval Inquisition did not function was Castile, for in the sixteenth century the Spanish Inquisition was extremely active there. A high proportion of the population of Castile in the Middle Ages were Muslims and Jews, and religious toleration formed an important and necessary part of government policy. Alphonso the Wise (1252—84) styled himself the king of the three religions. Although he enacted severe laws against heretics, ordering that all those who would not recant should be burnt, he would not allow the Inquisition to be set up in his kingdom, perhaps fearing that it would disturb the religious equilibrium he was trying to establish.

Unlike the later Spanish and Roman Inquisitions, the medieval Inquisition possessed no central organization to co-ordinate and direct the activities of its various provinces. Sometimes one particularly gifted inquisitor would be appointed inquisitor-general for several provinces by the pope, and would be given authority over the other inquisitors in that area, but normally each province was autonomous, and each inquisitor was responsible to the pope for the conduct of his office. This had two important consequences, both of which were detrimental to the efficiency of the organization as a whole. First, there was no recognized means of communication between different provinces: two inquisitors in neighbouring provinces might arrange to co-operate and to exchange information, but they were not required to do so, and it was thus easier for heretics to escape detection by fleeing from one jurisdiction to another. Secondly, it was quite possible for an idle inquisitor to do nothing, since the pope obviously did not have the time personally to supervise the work of every province, yet there was no department of the curia analogous to the later Holy Office whose duty it was to do so.

Robert 'le bougre' in France

Pope Gregory IX, the founder of the Inquisition, tried to appoint inquisitors in all parts of western Europe where Catharism was known to exist. One such area was northern France, for although Catharism was not so widely diffused there as in the south, it had existed in some parts of the north for a long time and had proved very persistent. In 1233 the pope empowered some of the Dominicans of Besancon to make inquisition at Charité-sur-Loire, where heresy had proved particularly difficult to eradicate. Their leader was Robert, known as *le bougre,* or 'the Bulgar', because he was a converted Cathar. His intemperate zeal antagonized the bishops in whose dioceses he was working and in 1234 they persuaded the pope to withdraw his licence.

In the following year Gregory IX renewed Robert's commission, appointing him inquisitor general for the whole French kingdom, and ordering all bishops to assist him. His activities ranged over much of north-eastern France and he met with great success. There is little precise information available about the methods he used, but he seems to have preferred a public confrontation with suspects to the normal inquisitorial practice of a private

examination. Those who recanted were sentenced to public penance, while those who refused to do so were adjudged guilty and
were burnt. Robert's most notable achievement was to convict 183
perfected Cathars at Mont-Aimé in 1239, all of whom were burnt
at one mass execution. This took place in the presence of the king
of Navarre (the count of Champagne), the archbishop of Rheims
and 15 bishops, so clearly at this stage his measures enjoyed
the full support of the civil and ecclesiastical authorities. Yet
a few years later he was removed from office by the pope and
imprisoned by his own order until he died. The true reasons for this
are not known: chroniclers speak vaguely of his wicked deeds, but
do not specify what they were. It would certainly seem true that in
his later years his immoderate zeal and demagogic power com-
bined to make him find heresy where none existed, and to sentence
innocent people, and this may be sufficient reason to explain his
disgrace.

As a result of his fierce persecution Catharism in northern
France was driven underground, and its leaders went into exile in
those parts of Lombardy where heresy was still tolerated. Raynier
Sacconi, writing in *c*.1250, reported that there were about 150
northern French *perfecti* in Verona and its neighbourhood. St
Louis was anxious that heresy should not revive in his kingdom,
and in 1255 requested Pope Alexander IV to organize the Inquisition there on a proper institiutional basis. This was done, and the
inquisitors, who were Dominicans, are known to have been active
there in the second half of the thirteenth century. Their work is
very poorly documented, although it seems reasonable to suppose
that, like their colleagues in Languedoc, they were rooting out the
remnants of Cathar belief. There is no evidence of Cathar survival
in northern France after 1300.

Catharism had been active in Catalonia since the 1170s and
the kingdom of Aragon, of which Catalonia formed part, was an
obvious place of refuge for Cathars who wished to escape from
persecution in Languedoc. Gregory IX entrusted the work of
inquisition in Aragon to the mendicant orders in 1238, and the
procedure they were to follow was drawn up in 1242 by the council
of Tarragona on the advice of St Raymond of Peñafort. He was
one of the most distinguished canon lawyers of his age, and the
most eminent Aragonese churchman, for he was a former papal
Grand Penitentiary and a retired general of the Dominican order.
The Aragonese Inquisition appears in the course of the thirteenth
century to have succeeded in extirpating Catharism: certainly
when the last Cathar refugees fled there from Languedoc in the
early years of the fourteenth century they were not persecuted, but
they did not find any other Cathars there with whom they could

make contact. This suggests that the Inquisition had done its work so effectively that it was no longer vigilant for fresh outbreaks of heresy.

The kings of France and Aragon were willing to give their wholehearted support to the papacy in its battle against heresy, and to allow the inquisitors whom the holy see appointed to work freely in their states with the full co-operation of royal officals. The situation in the lands ruled by the Emperor Frederick II, which comprised Germany, Lombardy, Tuscany and the Sicilian kingdom, was very different. The emperor was no friend to heretics, but throughout much of his reign he was no friend to the papacy either and was unwilling to allow the papal Inquisition to work in his dominions.

Conrad of Marburg in Germany

His opposition might not have proved a diriment impediment to the pope in Germany, where imperial power was very weak. Indeed, it used to be thought that the first evidence of anything like an inquisitorial appointment was that made by Gregory IX on 12 June 1227, empowering Conrad of Marburg to act as a kind of inquisitor-general for Germany. Conrad was a secular priest and had been the confessor of St Elizabeth of Thuringia. H.C.Lea aptly described him thus: 'Stern in temper and narrow in mind, his bigotry was ardent to the pitch of insanity'. (H.C.Lea, *A History of the Inquisition in the Middle Ages,* 3 vols, New York, 1888, II, p. 326). Kieckhefer has pointed out that there is no firm evidence that Conrad received more than papal licence to act as an episcopal inquisitor. In that case his activities would not concern us, but some examination of them is necessary because he influenced the development of the papal Inquisition in one significant way.

Conrad certainly had nothing in common with the careful legalism of his southern French and Italian colleagues. His method of making inquisition was to rouse a mob, to round up suspects with their help, and to offer them the choice of recantation or death. The usual punishment meted out to the penitent was shaving the head. There was no semblance of a trial, and large numbers of victims perished in his two years of active ministry (1231—3). There seem at that time to have been no Cathars in Germany, and Conrad's energies were devoted chiefly to unmasking Luciferans. He believed, and persuaded the pope to believe, that there were organized groups of devil-worshippers in Germany, who had sold their souls to Lucifer. In return the prince of darkness manifested himself to them in varying guises, including that of a gigantic cat. Having become morally depraved in this way these sectaries abandoned themselves to promiscuous sexual orgies. The existence of heretics of the kind Conrad described seems highly doubtful, although there may have been, as H.C.Lea conjectured, some people in Germany at that time who held the Origenist view that even the devil would ultimately be saved. It is, moreover, difficult to see why anybody should have resorted to such extreme measures in order to enjoy amusements which were readily available in any fair-sized German town. But as a result of Conrad's dynamic personality and zealous fanaticism many, presumably innocent, people suffered, until he made the tactical mistake of impugning a nobleman, the count of Seyn, who was powerful enough to force him to resign. Soon after this Conrad was murdered.

His activities probably do not form part of the history of the Inquisition, but his descriptions of the errors of the Luciferans were repeated by Gregory IX in instructions to the German authorities, and thus were copied in the papal registers. They could then be used, as M.C.Barber has shown in his *Trial of the Templars,* to discredit other groups whom the authorities considered suspect. One minor consequence of Conrad's anti-Luciferan propaganda was that the cat, previously esteemed in western Europe as a means of rat control, acquired an undeserved reputation, which it retained for centuries, as an associate of sorcerers.

After Conrad's death Gregory IX did not appoint any papal inquisitors in Germany. This was probably the result of a number of different factors: the unwillingness of the emperor to co-oprate; the absence of Cathars in Germany; and the general revulsion produced by the excesses of Conrad of Marburg who, although he may not have been in the strict sense a papal inquisitor, certainly had the pope's licence to act as an episcopal inquisitor. After the death of Frederick II's son, Conrad IV, in 1254, some members of the mendicant orders were given inquisitorial authority in Germany by the popes, but they did not develop institutional powers, like their French and Aragonese colleagues, and the Inquisition was not fully established in Germany until the fourteenth century.

Inquisitors in Italy

The Inquisition could not, of course, be introduced in the Sicilian kingdom in Frederick II's lifetime, because his authority there was assured. There were some Cathars in southern Italy, and the emperor prosecuted a few of them, but there was no systematic persecution in his reign.

Lombardy and Tuscany traditionally formed part of the Empire and the Cathars were particularly active there: indeed, as has been seen in the last chapter, the Cathar churches of Languedoc set up their headquarters in Lombardy when the Inquisition became too oppressive in their homeland. Both Lombardy and Tuscany were dominated by self-governing city republics, many of which were bitterly hostile to the emperor, who spent much of his reign trying to subdue them. Although the pope was their natural ally, many of the anti-imperial cities were unwilling to enforce papal laws against heresy, partly because they were jealous of their independence, but mainly because the Cathars were supported by some of the chief families in most cities, so that any attempt to suppress them was bound to cause faction. There was, of course, no question of enforcing the heresy laws in those regions which obeyed Frederick II.

Unpromising though the situation seemed, Gregory IX was not deterred from taking action. The earliest known instance of the appointment of a papal inquisitor relates to Florence. The Cathar bishop of that city had been arrested by the lay authorities in 1226, had recanted his errors and had been set at liberty. He immediately relapsed into heresy and was arrested again, and, when the pope was consulted about what action to take, he nominated the Dominican prior of Sta Maria Novella as inquisitor to examine the offender. The outcome was something of an anti-climax, as the Cathar bishop escaped from prison during his trial and was never recaptured.

Despite this setback the office of inquisitor was perpetuated in Florence, and in 1232 the pope also appointed inquisitors in those parts of Lombardy which were willing to co-operate with him. Although some *perfecti* were brought to trial and, if they refused to recant, were burnt by the secular authorities, the inquisitors could not work systematically for the reasons already given. The successful launching of the Italian Inquisition was largely the work of a single Dominican, Peter of Verona. While acting as inquisitor in Lombardy he had persuaded the Milanese authorities to burn some *perfecti* whom he had tried, and in 1244 he was called in to assist the work of the Inquisition in Florence. The inquisitors there knew who the Cathars were, but could not take action against them because they had patrons among some of the powerful families in the city. Peter of Verona found a simple but effective solution to this *impasse*. He rallied Catholic support, particularly among the nobility, and founded a religious society called *La Compagnia della Fede*. This was, in effect, a Catholic gang, which beat up its Cathar rivals in a series of street battles in August 1245. The work of Inquisition could then proceed smoothly. Peter returned to Lombardy, and continued to prosecute heretics there until he was assassinated by some of their supporters in 1252. In less than a year he was canonized and, as St Peter Martyr, he became the first saint that the Inquisition had produced.

His work in Lombardy was taken over by another Dominican, Raynier Sacconi, a converted Cathar minister (it is not known whether he had been a bishop or a deacon). The Emperor Frederick had died in 1250, but the Inquisition in Lombardy was still impeded in its work by his son, Conrad IV. When Conrad in his turn died in 1254, Pope Innocent IV thought that imperial opposition in Italy would collapse, and, in expectation of this, he systematically organized the Inquisition throughout Italy. The Dominicans were left in charge of Lombardy, but the Franciscans were entrusted with the work in Tuscany, central Italy and the Sicilian kingdom. These preparations proved to be premature, since Frederick II's illegitimate son, Manfred, gained control of Sicily, while his supporter, Ezzolino of Romagna, remained powerful in eastern Lombardy. Since both were implacably opposed to the pope, the Inquisition could not operate in those areas. Ezzolino's death in 1259 was no help to the Inquisition, because his territory was taken over by Uberto Pallavicini of Cremona, who was also an ally of Manfred's, and who extended his power to western Lombardy by gaining control of Milan.

The Inquisition continued to function where it was allowed to do so, but it is clear from the writings of Raynier Sacconi that it was not proving very effective. Raynier was appointed inquisitor-general of Lombardy in 1257 by Pope Alexander IV, but there were many, perhaps a majority, of places within the area of his offical jurisdiction where he could not operate. Raynier estimated that there were 2,550 perfected Cathars in Lombardy and Tuscany at that time, and he was in a position to be well informed about this because he had been an ordained minister in the Cathar church. He also computed that there were less than 200 *perfecti* affiliated to the southern French churches at the same time, and although his information about Languedoc may have been less accurate, the fact that he supposed that there were roughly twelve times as many perfected Cathars in Lombardy as in southern Franced does suggest that the Lombard Inquisition was not working nearly so effectively as its counterpart in Languedoc.

The political situation in Italy changed radically in 1266 when, at the suggestion of the pope, Charles of Anjou, brother of St Louis of France, brought an army there, defeated Manfred and became king of Sicily. His opponents looked for leadership to Frederick II's grandson, the 16-year-old Conradin, who invaded Italy in 1268, but this venture was unsuccessful and he was slain. The death of Uberto Pallavicini later that year marked the end of effective opposition to Charles of Anjou in northern Italy also.

Charles had come to power with the support of the pope and in return he aided the pope to the full in the suppression of heresy. The Inquisition was established in the Sicilian kingdom in 1269, and Charles gave military aid to the holy see, where necessary, to enforce the acceptance of the heresy laws on the cities of north and central Italy. Consequently the Inquisition could finally begin to function efficiently throughout Italy. The republic of Venice held out longest: it refused to admit inquisitors at all until 1289 and even after that time supervised their work closely, but elsewhere the Inquisition met with no impediment. Initially quite large numbers of *perfecti* were discovered. 174 of them were arrested at Sirmione in 1276, for example: they all refused to recant, and were burnt, the last Cathar bishop of Toulouse probably being one of their number.

Catharism thus became an underground movement in Italy, just as it had already done in Languedoc. The inquisitors showed their customary willingness to reconcile the penitent, and burnings in Italy, as elsewhere, were normally reserved for *perfecti* who refused to recant. This was true of the majority of them, but any of the perfect who did recant were treated with great leniency. This was often of benefit to the Inquisition, as the career of Raynier Sacconi shows, but such clemency could have quite the opposite effect. Armanno Pungilupo of Ferrara, for example, was a perfected Cathar who recanted before the inquisitors in 1254 and was released. He became an exemplary Catholic, but, unknown to the Church authorities, he had secretly relapsed and been reconsoled by the Cathar bishop. His services to the Cathar church were immense, because, as a Catholic of good repute, he was, for example, allowed to visit prisoners of the Inquisition in need of spiritual help. Yet he was outwardly so devout in his Catholic observance that after his death in 1269 a popular cult developed at his tomb in Ferrara cathedral. The Inquisition, who later received much information about his activities as a crypto-Cathar while they were interrogating other suspects, tried to suppress expressions of popular devotion to him, but local feeling was so strong that they did not succeed until 1301, when finally their evidence was accepted, by Boniface VIII, and Armanno's tomb was broken open and his bones publicly burnt.

By about 1320 Catharism had virtually disappeared from Italy, and the reasons for its collapse there were probably much the same as those which led to its annihilation in Languedoc. In Italy, as in France, the Inquisition was given the credit for this, although in both cases the extent of its contribution to the eradication of Catharism is uncertain. Some Italian Cathars sought refuge in Corsica, and survived there until the 1370s, but Corsica was remote not only from the Inquisition, but also from the other religious and intellectual movements which proved inimical to Catharism. Although some cases of alleged Catharism came to light on the Italian mainland in the second half of the fourteenth century, the people concerned seem mostly to have belonged to Waldensian communities which had absorbed some Cathar teachings at an earlier date. A solitary outbreak of genuine Catharism occurred in 1388 at Chieri, near Turin, but this was the result of a mission conducted by a *perfectus* from Bosnia.

The Cathar faith continued to be practised openly in Bosnia until the Turkish conquest in 1463. This was technically a Catholic country, but, except in the coastal cities, Catholicism had never taken a firm hold on the mass of the population, and there was little check to the spread of Catharism there in the later Middle Ages. The holy see preached crusades against the heretical Bosnians from the thirteenth century onwards: these normally took the form of invasions by the kings of Hungary, but they achieved little beyond securing the nominal, and often temporary, adherence of the Bosnian rulers to the Roman faith. The popes also, from time to time, empowered members of the mendicant orders to act as inquisitors in Bosnia, but they were powerless in a country where the mass of the population was sympathetic to Catharism, where there was little Catholic organization, and where the Cathar leaders enjoyed the patronage of the nobility and often of the crown as well. Yet although it was so close to Italy, Bosnia did not pose a threat to the work of the Inquisition there. It may have been used as a place of refuge by persecuted Italian Cathars, but, except for the isolated example which I have mentioned, there is no evidence that the Bosnian Cathars ever sent missionaries to Italy. This lack of contact may reflect a language difficulty, since the Bosnians were Slav speakers, but it probably also reflects a lack of evangelical fervour on the part of the Bosnian Cathar church in this period.

After the Cathars had been suppressed in Italy the Inquisition remained as an established part of society throughout the peninsula. There, as in France, it seemed to have proved its worth as an agent for eradicating heresy, while the presence of the Bosnian Cathars across the Adriatic suggested that vigilance was still necessary to prevent any recurrence of the evil. It was probably because the Inquisition had appeared to meet with such success in France and Italy that in the course of the fourteenth century it became established also in parts of Europe where it had never functioned before. Inquisitors were appointed in Poland and Bohemia in 1318, and in Portugal in 1376, and the Inquisition also became firmly grounded in Germany. Yet perhaps the most convincing evidence that there is that the Inquisition had come to be regarded as a normal part of Catholic life by the fourteenth century is contained in letters written to the pope by missionaries belonging to the mendicant orders. In several cases friars working in north Africa and Asia assure the pontiff that they have appointed inquisitors. Such officials, living in the lands of the sultan of Morocco or the ilkhan of Persia, cannot have exercised the same powers as their European colleagues, but they had been appointed, it would seem, because the office of inquisitor had come to be regarded as part of the normal establishment of any province of the Church.

8

Prosecutions of the fourteenth century

The Knights Templar

As the Inquisition's fight against Catharism drew to a close in the early years of the fourteenth century, it was called upon to investigate reports of other kinds of heresy. The first major work of this sort which it undertook was to bring the Knights Templar to trial. They belonged to the oldest of the military orders, and were men who lived under monastic vows but who, instead of devoting their lives to prayer, were pledged to a life of active service, fighting the infidel. Founded in 1119 to protect pilgrim routes in the Holy Land, the order of the Temple spread rapidly and became one of the chief military supports of the Crusader States, but also defended the frontiers of Christendom both in Spain and in eastern Europe. The order was exempted by the pope from obedience to any ecclesiastical authority save that of the holy see, and it acquired great wealth through donations of landed property throughout the western world. The Templars also found means of circumventing the Church's usury laws, and became important bankers, an activity which centred on the Paris house of their order. They were highly esteemed by their Muslim enemies both for their courage and for their integrity. The loss of Frankish territory in Syria in 1291, however, deprived them of their principal justification, yet they retained their extensive lands, mostly situated in western Europe.

In 1307 King Philip IV of France claimed that the Inquisitor of the realm, William of Paris, had informed him that the Templars were corrupt. It was alleged that postulants at their reception into the order were required to deny Christ, to spit on the cross, and to kiss the anus of the officer who presided at the service. It was further maintained that the order enjoined sodomy on its members, and that in chapter the brethren worshipped an idol in the form of a head. The king professed himself to be greatly scandalized by these revelations and ordered his officials to arrest all the brethren in France on 13 October 1307. The charges made against the Templars bear a remarkable resemblance to those made by Conrad of Marburg against the fictitious Luciferans a century earlier, as M.C.Barber has pointed out, and they would seem to have been as little grounded in fact as the earlier accusations. No doubt among the Templars, as among other military groups in most ages, there were individual cases of homosexuality and of blasphemy; but it is scarcely credible that an order whose members hazarded their lives in defence of the Christian faith should corporately have apostatized from it.

Although the Inquisition of France formally brought the charges against the Templars, there seems no doubt that Philip IV was the real instigator of the trial. As was seen in chapter 6, the king had, since the 1290s, been trying to reduce the powers of the Inquisition, and it would appear that by 1307 he had succeeded in bringing it under royal control. The Templars could not be accused in bishops' courts, since they were exempt from episcopal jurisdiction, but they were not exempt from the Inquisition, which represented the pope himself. Whether the king believed the allegations made against the Templars it is impossible to tell, but he certainly stood to gain by the downfall of the order, not least because he was deeply in the debt of the Paris Temple. His officials were instructed to arrest the Templars throughout France, to imprison them, and to extract from them confessions of their guilt in respect of the charges brought against them; the obdurate were, if necessary, to be tortured, and threatened with death if they persisted in denying the allegations. Only then were they to be handed over to the inquisitors for examination in accordance with canon law. Only in the case of the Grand Master, James of Molay, and the chief officers of the order did the Inquisition conduct all the preliminary examinations. They were interrogated by the inquisitor of France, William of Paris, and, with few exceptions, made the required confessions. It is assumed that the inquisitor used torture, or the threat of torture, against these men, as he was empowered to do when dealing with the obdurate. The Inquisition's greatest service to the crown was to secure these confessions from the leaders of the order, since this did more than anything else to make credible the accusations which had been levelled against the brethren of the Temple.

Pope Clement V did not at first believe that the confessions were true, and also saw that because the Templars were an international order their fate could not be decided by French tribunals alone. In 1308 he revoked the power of the Inquisition to hear the case, and instead appointed eight commissioners to investigate the charges made against the order as a whole, while entrusting the investigation of individual cases to episcopal commissions, which were to be composed of the bishop, two canons of his cathedral, two Dominicans and two Franciscans. In making this ruling the pope, implicitly at least, revoked the privileges which exempted the Templars from episcopal authority. The episcopal tribunals could operate throughout the western world, even in those countries like England where there was no Inquisition, and the pope ordered all rulers to arrest and examine the Templars in their dominions.

The French crown controlled the episcopate as firmly as it did the Inquisition, so that this change in procedure was of no help in securing the Templars a fairer trial. Bishops' courts had the same power as Inquisition courts to try heretics and the same right to sentence them. Hitherto, only the Inquisition had been allowed to use torture, but in the case of the Templars the pope granted that privilege to the episcopal tribunals also. The papal commissioners meanwhile sat in Paris and invited the Templars to come forward if they wished to defend the order. Over 500 of them volunteered to do so, but were discouraged from appearing by the action of Philip of Marigny, archbishop of Sens, and brother of Philip IV's finance minister. He condemned 54 Templars in his jurisdiction as relapsed heretics, because they had retracted their original confessions, and handed them over to the secular arm to be burnt. This was an abuse of language as well as of justice: the term 'relapsed heretic' described somebody who, having abjured his errors, subsequently resumed his heretical practice; it had never been used by the Inquisition to mean a heretic who recanted but subsequently affirmed that he had been innocent all the time. But Philip of Marigny was not an inquisitor, and these burnings were the work of a provincial synod. They effectively deterred any other Templars from trying to defend the order: they could not do so without retracting their confessions, and that had been shown to be a suicidal action to take.

In accordance with the pope's orders the Templars outside France were arrested by the secular authorities and examined by episcopal tribunals. In some countries,like Aragon, inquisitors were called in to advise the court, but the trials were conducted by bishops, not by the Inquisition. At their discretion, and by special papal indult, the bishops were empowered to order the torturing of obdurate prisoners. In England, the government of Edward II was very slow in obeying papal injunctions, and in 1309 the abbot of Lagny, near Paris, and a canon of Narbonne were sent there by the pope to conduct investigations. Although they are usually referred to as inquisitors, they do not seem to have held inquisitorial commissions. They acted in conjunction with the English bishops, and were exasperated by the inability, or unwillingness, of the English authorities to torture suspects. It is, perhaps, significant that no confessions of any substance were made by the Templars of England.

The final decision about the fate of the order was made in a general council of the Church which met at Vienne in 1312. The order was dissolved, and its property was given to the other great military order, the Hospitallers. It was decreed that those knights who had been found innocent (as some had), together with those who had confessed and recanted their errors, should be set free, and be assigned a pension from the revenues of the order. Those who had been found guilty but had not repented should suffer the rigours of the laws against heretics, and the pope reserved to himself the cases of the Grand Master and of three other officers of the order. They were finally examined at Paris in 1314 by three cardinals, representing the pope, and a council of the French church. The Grand Master and the Master of Normandy retracted their confessions and asserted their innocence. The council passed no judgement on them, but that same evening the two Templar leaders were burnt alive by the orders of Philip IV.

The part played by the Inquisition in the trial of the Templars was slight but significant. It initiated the proceedings, and by the use of torture it extracted damaging confessions from the officers of the order which made the charges seem credible. Ordinary knights were, in most cases, tortured and forced to confess by royal officials, so that the inquisitors were merely required to give official recognition to these admissions of guilt. In 1308 Pope Clement removed the trial from the Inquisition and entrusted it to episcopal tribunals and to papal commissioners. The burnings which took place were the work of episcopal tribunals, not of the Inquisition, and so was the torturing of suspects.

Yet although its part in the trial was slight the Inquisition had proved its worth to the French crown. The property of the Temple was transferred to the Hospitallers, but this did not happen until the French crown had secured the cancellation of all its debts to the Paris Temple and been paid 310,000 *livres tournois* by the Hospitallers for the expenses involved in administering the property during the years of the trial. It was popularly supposed that the Hospitallers of France were poorer after they had received the gift of the Templars' estates than they had been before. Philip IV had shown that the Inquisition in France had become a tool of Capetian government, and its place in the kingdom was henceforth assured. It was not used again in the Middle Ages on so large a scale for such a blatantly political purpose.

Followers of the 'Free Spirit'

While the trial of the Templars was in progress the inquisitor of Paris burnt a woman named Marguerite Porete because she refused to recant certain teachings she had published in a book called *The Mirror of Simple Souls,* which the theology faculty of the University of Paris deemed heretical. The condemned teachings were manifestations of the heresy of the Free Spirit. Those who held this faith aimed at achieving perfection and union with God in this life: this objective was orthodox. However, they also asserted that perfection was a personal matter which concerned only the individual soul and God, and that the mediation of the Church on earth or of the angels and saints in Heaven was unnecessary, and such a view was heretical. Their orthodox opponents represented them as holding that a soul which has attained perfection in this life is no longer bound by the moral law, but may do what it will: it has become, in fact, a free spirit. The implications of this opinion were viewed with alarm by puritans, of whom the Church in all ages has always had its fair share.

It used to be thought that there was an organized sect of the Brethren of the Free Spirit, but recent scholars, notably Lerner, in his *The Heresy of the Free Spirit in the Later Middle Ages,* have argued convincingly that this was not so. These opinions were held by individuals, all of whom were concerned with attaining mystical experience, and some of whom influenced others through their writings or their practice. The heresy does not seem to have had a particular founder, and attempts to connect it with early-thirteenth-century thinkers, like Ortlieb of Strasburg, have proved unsuccessful. Its existence is first securely attested in Swabia by St Albert the Great, writing 1261—80. It was not in any sense a popular movement, or at all widely diffused, and its supporters seem to have been literate people, drawn chiefly from the middle and upper classes.

In 1307 the archbishop of Cologne claimed that he had discovered this heresy among beguines and beghards in his diocese, and prosecuted some of them. Beguines and beghards were members of lay religious communities which had sprung up all over western Europe since the mid eleventh century. Beghards were communities of men, beguines communities of women. Their members shared a common life, but took no vows and were free to leave and to marry at any time. Each foundation had its rule of life and was directed by a religious superior. The communities performed charitable works, but some of their members led lives devoted to contemplative prayer. Their constitutions made such communities possible centres of unorthodox opinions, and the report of the archbishop of Cologne led the papacy to associate these communities in Germany with the heresy of the Free Spirit. The Council of Vienne in 1312 condemned that heresy, and stated that it was prevalent among German beguines and beghards.

Consequently communities of this kind were subject to sporadic persecution by the lay and ecclesiastical authorities in Germany, but the Inquisition played no part in this because it had not been established there. This was remedied by Pope Urban V, who in 1364 divided Germany into four provinces and appointed Dominican inquisitors to serve them, with specific instructions to deal with the beghards and the beguines. In 1369 the emperor Charles IV extended protection to the inquisitors under the laws of the empire and empowered them to confiscate houses of beghards for use as prisons, and to sell beguinages and divide the profits between local charities, local town councils and the Inquisition. The inquisitor Walter Kerlinger vigorously prosecuted these communities in north-eastern Germany from 1366 to 73. Some adopted the tertiary rule of one of the mendicant orders to escape dissolution, but many were disbanded. The Inquisition expected to find evidence of the heresy of the Free Spirit among members of these communities and used set forms of interrogation to question them. Such a method, which had proved invaluable when examining Cathars, was quite inappropriate in the case of beguines and beghards. The heresy of the Free Spirit was concerned with subtle theological speculations about the nature and operation of grace. Many of the beguines and beghards, who were innocent of heresy, and who had received no scholastic training in theology, found it hard to give orthodox answers, or even, in some cases, to understand the questions. Some, it would seem, took the easy way out, and confessed to errors which they did not hold and to moral turpitude of which they had not been guilty, recanted these imaginary errors, and were given canonical penances. The inquisitors were thus confirmed in their suspicion that an insidious heresy was at work, centred in these lay communities, which was subversive of orthodox belief and of soical ethics. In the course of their investigations they did, of course, find some people who were truly believers in the Free Spirit and were prepared to be martyred for their opinions: whatever views they may in theory have held about the impeccability of the perfected soul, they seldom confessed to moral failings and seem, on the whole, to have been extremely high-minded.

In the latter part of the fourteenth century the persecution of beguines and beghards died down, and it was halted completely in the early fifteenth century when the Council of Constance gave its approval to orthodox communities of this kind. Prosecutions of adherents of the Free Spirit became very rare at the same time, and ceased completely in the fifteenth century. Because it had interpreted individual deviations from orthodoxy as symptoms of organized heresy, the Church had, in the case of the Free Spirit, marshalled the Inquisition to fight an enemy which did not exist. Many innocent beghards and beguines suffered as a result, for although few of them were sentenced to more than canonical penances, many of them were left destitute when the communities in which they lived were disbanded. The beguines and beghards might never have attracted systematic persecution at all had those of southern France not shown sympathy with the Spiritual Franciscans and thereby incurred the suspicion of the papacy.

The Spiritual Franciscans

St Francis's lofty ideals of complete poverty and total simplicity for his followers had been modified even in his lifetime, under papal direction, to enable the order to function more smoothly as part of the institutional Church. When he died in 1226 Francis left a Testament in which he set out his ideals for the order. Although this had no constitutional authority, it was treated with great reverence by some of his followers. In the thirteenth century, therefore, a division occurred in the order between those friars who were willing to modify the rule of poverty, and to accept privileges for the order, who were known as Conventuals, and the idealists, who wished to preserve the identity of the order as St Francis had conceived it, who were knows as Spirituals.

The Spirituals were greatly influenced by the writings of Joachim of Fiore, who had died in 1202 before their order was founded. He had taught that there were three ages of the world: that of the Father, which had lasted until the coming of Christ; that of the Son, in which he lived; and that of the Holy Spirit, which would succeed it. The Spirituals found passages in his works which seemed to prophesy the foundation of their own order, and to identify it as one of the portents which would occur before the beginning of the Age of the Spirit. They also noted that Joachim had taught that, before the Third Age came to pass, antichrist would come and would persecute the faithful. The Spirituals became powerful in the Franciscan province of Provence, which included much of Languedoc, and also in the March of Ancona, and they influenced lay people among whom they lived, particularly the beguines.

When the papacy moved to Avignon in the early fourteenth century it could not ignore the quarrel between the Spirituals and the Conventuals which was destroying the peace of the Franciscan order in Languedoc and attracting supporters among the laity. Many of the Spirituals refused obedience to their Conventual superiors on the grounds that they were disregarding the founder's Testament. Moreover, the Spirituals, like St Francis himself, emphasized the importance of poverty in the life of Christian perfection, but they also asserted, in terms more absolute than those their founder had used, that Christ and His Apostles had exemplified this virtue in their lives, and the implication of this was that the Spirituals were following the Lord's teachings more correctly than the rest of His Church.

John XXII, who became pope in 1316, wished to find a rapid solution to this long-standing problem, but in his attempt to do so he showed a lack of judgement about the character of the Spirituals. Many of them did believe that the new Age of the Holy Spirit was about to dawn, and were therefore in no mood to compromise their convictions in the interests of administrative convenience. In 1317 the pope ordered the Spirituals to swear to obey their superiors about the kind of habit they should wear, and to accept the discretion of their superiors about the storage of grain and wine for use in emergencies. These matters struck at the heart of the problem: the Spirituals wore short, patched habits, as they believed St Francis had done, which were unlike the full habits of the Conventuals; and they also considered that it was contrary to the spirit of the rule to take thought for the morrow by storing food. Spirituals who refused to take the oath were tried by the Inquisition, and in 1318 four of them were burnt at Marseilles for denying that the pope had the right to require them to swear this particular oath. Pope John had provided the Spirituals with their first martyrs.

The enforcement of outward conformity, as the pope discovered, was no real solution to the problem, since even those Spirituals who took the oath continued to believe that their attitude to poverty represented not only the teaching of St Francis, but also that of Christ Himself. In 1322, therefore, John XXII declared that it was heresy to deny that the Lord and His Apostles had lawful ownership of those things which the Gospels state that they possessed. In the view of some of the Spirituals this doctrinal definition was proof that John XXII was antichrist, whose coming Joachim of Fiore had predicted. Not all of them were driven to take up so extreme a position, but many felt obliged to separate themselves from the rest of the Franciscan order as a result of the pope's measures. All these dissident Spirituals were collectively known as Fraticelli.

This name covers several groups. The most eminent, led by Michael of Cesena, a former Minister General of the order, sought refuge at Munich with the Emperor Louis of Bavaria. Although some of them were important thinkers, whose writings were influential, they obtained no popular following, and they were, of course, immune from persecution. Other Spirituals, under the leadership of Angelo of Clareno, left the Franciscan order, but had no wish to break with the Catholic Church. They formed eremitical communities in Italy, and although they were sometimes persecuted they survived into the sixteenth century when they were merged with the Observant Franciscans. They might not have been persecuted at all had they not been associated in the mind of the papal curia with a third group of Fraticelli. These friars broke with the Church completely, saying that it was wrong to remain in communion with antichrist and his followers. They made no innovations in doctrine or practice, but set up their own church, with its own bishops and priests. They were considered particularly dangerous by the papacy because they carried out pastoral work among the laity in the true Franciscan tradition. They were very influential in the March of Ancona, and were also, for a time in the fourteenth century, tolerated in the Angevin kingdom of Naples.

The papacy could scarcely be expected to countenance a movement which denounced the pope as antichrist and claimed to be the true church. Spiritual Franciscans of all kinds, together with their supporters, were forced to abandon their convictions or to suffer persecution by the Inquisition in southern France. Elsewhere all of them suffered some degree of persecution: one priest of the Fraticelli, for example, was burnt in Florence by the Inquisition in 1389 for refusing to recant his opinion that John XXII's doctrine of apostolic poverty was heresy and that John himself was antichrist. But the political conditions of fourteenth-century Italy made systematic persecution difficult, and it was not until Martin V restored papal power there in the 1420s that the active wing of the Fraticelli was rigorously attacked. In 1426 the pope gave general powers of inquisition against them to the leaders of the Observant Franciscans, St John of Capistrano and James of the March. Since these men were seeking to restore the Franciscan order to its pristine observance, they were particularly hostile to the Fraticelli, who claimed to be not only the true church on earth, but also the true heirs of St Francis. With the help of the secular authorities, the inquisitors waged war on the lay supporters of the Fraticelli in the March of Ancona, laying waste 31 villages in the process, and eroding the power-base of the dissidents. The movement never recovered from this persecution. Its last known adherents were tried by the Inquisition in Rome in 1466 and those who refused to recant were burnt.

It is difficult not to sympathize with the Fraticelli. They numbered among them men of uncommon holiness, and the principles they defended were those that had been most highly esteemed in St Francis himself. They were certainly more admirable than Christ's businesslike but worldly vicar, John XXII, and it is therefore tempting to suppose that they were right in their views about apostolic poverty, although the plain sense of the Gospels would seem to show that the pope's definition was factually correct. Yet for all their distinctively Franciscan virtues the Fraticelli were unlike their founder in one central way: St Francis had accepted the authority of the Church even when it conflicted with his own vision, and in that sense the Conventuals walked in the spirit of their founder and the Fraticelli did not. Yet with tactful handling the Fraticelli might all have remained within the Church as a separate religious order, which was what some of them, at least, wanted to happen. Persecution was ill-suited as a tool to deal with this problem, but by the fourteenth century the Church authorities had come to regard coercion as normal when they were confronted by obdurate dissenters. This acceptance of force as a universal solvent is a measure of the influence which the Inquisition had come to exercise over the whole western Church in the first century of its existence.

The Waldensians

Throughout this time the Waldensians continued to survive. In the thirteenth century the Inquisition, though not centrally interested in them, tried such of them as were brought to its notice, and devised interrogatories for Waldensian suspects. In the face of persecution they withdrew from Languedoc and Lombardy, but remained in the remoter parts of Piedmont, and spread to southern Italy and also to southern and eastern Germany. The Waldensians owed their survival largely, it would seem, to the fact that they were unobtrusive, and did not excite unfavourable comment from their Catholic neighbours. They were willing to have their children baptized in the Catholic faith; they occasionally went to Mass, although they were reluctant to make their communion; and they were usually punctilious in the payment of tithe. Their own itinerant clergy ministered to them, but outwardly the Waldensians looked like lukewarm Catholics and were therefore indistinguishable from many of the Catholics around them.

From time to time they were persecuted. In Germany a quite rigorous persecution of Waldensians took place betwen 1389 and 1401, but this was largely the work of bishops and the Inquisition played only a very minor part in it. The Waldensians were not usually severely punished: normally they recanted and were dismissed with a penance, and they were only in serious danger if they were brought before the courts for a second offence. In such cases, as relapsed heretics, they were liable to suffer imprisonment or even death. In Piedmont, where they were usually left in peace, a crusade was preached against them in 1488, but although it caused much damage and suffering it did not succeed in extirpating them.

Their survival is evidence of the lack of zeal shown by most fourteenth-century inquisitors. The Inquisition was established in all the lands where the Waldensians lived, yet it took no virtually no action against them. Such persecution as there was of Waldensians was initiated by bishops and lay rulers.

There was, indeed, comparatively little for most inquisitors to do once Catharism had collapsed. An occasional local heresy might develop, centring round a particular leader. The strangest of these was the cult of Guglielma, a devout widow of Milan, who died in 1281 and was buried in the Cistercian abbey of Chiaravalle. Her disciples believed that she was the Holy Spirit incarnate and that she would return to usher in the age of the Paraclete, when there would be a new gospel and a church ruled by a woman pope and female cardinals. The sect was investigated by the Inquisition three times, and its leaders were dismissed as harmless, but its activities could not be ignored any longer when, at Easter 1300, the woman pope-disignate celebrated Mass at Guglielma's tomb. All the sectaries were arrested and those who had earlier abjured were burnt. There were only about five relapsed heretics, and Guglielma's other followers were given very minor penances. This unexpected offshoot of Joachim of Fiore had no descent.

Compared to the ferment of heresy which had existed in the thirteenth century, the fourteenth was a very peaceful time for the Inquisition. The votaries of the Free Spirit were unorganized and had no popular following; the influence of the Fraticelli was confined to certain areas; while unorthodox groups, like the disciples of Guiglielma, were comparatively rare and attracted few followers. Many inquisitors spent their entire careers with no official business to do, and could undertake other duties, such as teaching theology. They sometimes proved useful to secular rulers, as the trial of the Templars proved in France. They were also sometimes used by the holy see in unexpected ways, as when, in 1343, the Inquisition of Florence was empowered to prosecute the banking firm of the Acciajuoli for failing to pay to the pope certain monies which had been deposited with it.

The chief problem which the Inquisition faced at that time was loss of revenue. The decline in heresy led to a parallel decline in the properties which lay rulers might confiscate and from which the expenses of the Inquisition had hitherto been met. In places where the Inquisition was institutionalized, like France and Italy, its expenses remained high, because it had buildings to maintain and employees to pay. In some Italian cities the inquisitors raised money by selling licences to carry arms to men who could not obtain permission to do so from the civic authorities, since the Inquisition was empowered to arm its retainers. Leaders of criminal gangs sometimes obtained licences in this way, and were presumably prepared to pay handsomely for them, until the abuse was stopped by strictly limiting the number of retainers whom the inquisitors were licensed to arm, as had been done in France from the beginning. Another example of the methods which inquisitors used to raise money is the ludicrous case, cited by Kieckhefer in his *Repression of Heresy in Medieval Germany,* of the inquisitor at Strasburg in 1399 who imposed a pilgrimage on a Waldensian penitent, but offered to perform the penance himself in return for three guldens because the accused had swollen feet. This is, indeed, a very different situation from that which had obtained a hundred years or more before in France and Italy, where the trials conducted by the Inquisition had led to the confiscation of property on a vast scale.

9
Sorcery and reform

In the fifteenth century the Inquisition became involved in a new range of work, the trial of sorcerers. Sorcery was an offence in canon law, but suspects were normally tried in the bishops' courts, and, indeed, in 1258 Pope Alexander IV had instructed inquisitors only to deal with withchcraft in cases in which it was manifestly connected with heresy. In 1398, however, the theology faculty of the University of Paris determined that acts of sorcery accomplished by means of a tacit or explicit pact with the devil entailed apostasy from the Christian faith and were therefore to be considered heretical. As a result, withchcraft came within the jurisdiction of the Inquisition. Kieckhefer has advanced the interesting argument that this change in attitude towards witchcraft came about because men educated in the Aristotelian tradition looked for an efficient cause of the results alleged to have been produced by sorcery. Being Christian, they could ascribe those results only to the intervention of the devil, since they could no longer accept them as simple magical occurrences, as less reflective people had hitherto done.

Even without this new ruling, the Inquisition would probably have been required to conduct the trial of Joan of Arc. Captured in battle by the English and Burgundians in 1430, she was examined by the bishop of Beauvais, in conjunction with John le Maître, deputy inquisitor of Rouen for the inquisitor of France. The French Inquisition, with its headquarters in Paris, was, at this stage in the Hundred Years' War, under English political control. Joan claimed that her military career had been inspired by Sts Catherine and Margaret, and was condemned by the court for persisting in this opinion and burnt at Rouen in 1431. In one sense this was a political judgement, since it was in the interests of the English to secure the death of this woman who had taken a leading part in stimulating French resistance to their rule. English scholars of an older generation, who praised English kings for refusing to allow the Inquisition to be established in their realm, tended to gloss over the way in which Henry VI's government invoked the help of the Inquisition against Joan of Arc with as few qualms as Philip IV had shown when invoking its aid against the Templars. Nevertheless, it is also true that a claim to personal revelation such as Joan made would probably have involved her in trouble with the Church authorities at some time in her life, while the strange advice that the virgin saints were alleged to have given her, to dress in men's attire, must have led her judges to suspect diabolical intervention, irrespective of the political pressures which were brought to bear on them. Joan is one of the very few people condemned by the Inquisition whose sentence was subsequently reversed by the holy see. Pope Calixtus III quashed the sentence in 1456, and Joan has since achieved the position, unique among all those whom the Inquisition ordered to be burnt, of being venerated as a saint by the entire Catholic world.

The other celebrated case of sorcery with which the Inquisition was required to deal in the fifteenth century was that of Gilles de Rais, Marshal of France. He appears, from his own confession, to have been a psychopathic pederast, who found sexual satisfaction in seducing and murdering young boys. In addition, he practised alchemy, and this laid him open to charges of sorcery and diabolism. It was the latter offence which led to his trial being conducted by the Inquisition. His case was heard by the bishop of Nantes, and by John Blouyn, vicar of the Inquisitor of France, to whom he freely admitted his guilt, after his servants, under torture, had betrayed his secrets. He was handed over to the secular arm and was hanged in 1440. His body was then partially burnt before being given Christian burial, for he had died repentant. Although his trial may have been engineered by his political enemies, there is no reason to doubt that his confession was substantially true. His condemnation may, perhaps, be considered an unusual instance of the acceptable face of the Inquisition. Few people, it may reasonably be assumed, would contend that he should have been allowed to continue murdering the innocent, yet no court which did not use the ruthless methods of the Inquisition could have secured the conviction of a man of his eminence.

Although more cases of witchcraft were brought before the Inquisition in the fifteenth century than previously, the total number was insignificant when compared with the mass trials which took place in what are sometimes mistakenly considered the more enlightened ages of the sixteenth and seventeenth centuries. Nevertheless, the medieval Inquisition made a malign bequest to posterity in the form of the *Malleus Maleficarum*, or 'Hammer of Witches', published in 1486 by the Dominican inquisitors Henry Krämer and Jacob Sprenger. This encyclopaedic work was used as a source-book about witchcraft by Catholic and Protestant witch-hunters of later ages, and caused far more damage than the witch-hunt conducted by Krämer himself at Innsbruck in 1485. His activities were fairly efficiently impeded by the local bishop, who referred to him as 'quite childish, on account of old age'.

Sorcery could have been dealt with in most instances by the episcopal courts, as had previously been the custom, and the Inquisition could have confined its activities to its traditional task of dealing with heresy. When a serious outbreak of heresy did occur in the fifteenth century, that of the Hussite revolt in Bohemia, the Inquisition proved powerless to deal with it. The Inquisition had been established in Prague since 1318 and had taken no action against John Hus when he pursued his public ministry there. He was, it would seem, completely orthodox in faith, and was concerned to reform abuses in the Church. Even his use of Wycliffe's writings was not at the time heretical, because, although some of the English thinker's propositions had been condemned by a synod in London, no judgement had been pronouned on them by the holy see. Thus when Hus went to the Council of Constance in 1415 to defend himself against his critics, he was given a certificate of orthodox belief by the inquisitor of Prague. This did not prove any more protection to him than the safe-conduct issued by the Emperor Sigismund. He was examined by the Council and condemned to death by burning because, when required to abjure certain errors in his teaching, he made the cardinal mistake of appealing from a General council of the Church to the authority of Holy Scripture. This was perhaps the only sense in which he may be considered a proto-Protestant. His trial does not concern us, since the Inquisition played no part in it, but the consequences are of relevance to the work of that tribunal.

His death sparked off a revolt against the Church among his followers in Bohemia, but this received such wide support that the Inquisition was powerless to act. The radical wing of the Hussite movement, the Taborites, were so militant that only armed force would have ensured their suppression, and their power was eventually broken in that way in 1434. The moderate Hussites, on the other hand, who were known as Utraquists, were so powerful and numerous that the authorities preferred to negotiate with them rather than to attempt to coerce them into conformity. After 1436 they were protected by the Bohemian crown, although the holy see never accorded them its recognition, but they might more justly be considered schismatics than heretics, since they were distinguished from Catholics only by their insistence on making their communion in both kinds, which was why they were called Utraquists.

An ironical situation therefore existed in fifteenth century

Europe. The Inquisition was established in Bohemia but could take no action against dissidents, who were protected by the crown. In England, on the other hand, where there was no Inquisition, Lollards, who held those teachings of Wycliffe which had been condemned as heretical, were burnt by act of parliament. Religious toleration, therefore, was not necessarily greater in those countries where the Inquisition did not function.

By the late fifteenth century the Inquisition had become dormant throughout most of Europe. Inquisitors continued to be appointed, but often they had no cases to try throughout their term of office. This moribund institution was brought back to life again by Queen Isabella of Castile, who was zealous to deal with Jewish and Muslim converts to Christianity among her subjects, who were suspected of clandestinely continuing to practise their old beliefs. The Inquisition had never operated in Castile, but in 1478 the queen received permission from Pope Sixtus IV to institute it there. The Castilian Inquisition was different from other provinces of the Inquisition in that the inquisitors were appointed by the crown, and could be dismissed without reference to the pope. The Inquisition in Castile thus became a department of royal government. In 1481—2 Isabella's husband, Ferdinand IV of Aragon, received permission from Rome to reform the Inquisition in his kingdom along similar lines. At this stage the Inquisitions in the two adjacent states remained idependent of each other, but this soon changed. In 1483 the *Consejo de la Suprema y General Inquisición,* commonly referred to as the *Suprema,* was set up to direct the Inquisition in Castile, under the presidency of the inquisitor-general, the Dominican friar Torquemada. Soon afterwards the pope nominated Torquemada inquisitor-general in Aragon also and the Aragonese Inquisition was brought under the authority of the *Suprema* in Castile.

The Inquisition was extended to all the dependencies of Spain, including, in the sixteenth century, those in the New World, and its work was directed by the *Suprema* and the inquisitor-general. Although it was an ecclesiastical tribunal, it was controlled by the Spanish crown, and it came to have great influence because it was the only institution whose jurisdiction was acknowledge throughout the Spanish Empire. It differed from the medieval Inquisition in that the activities of its constituent provinces were directed by a central authority which co-ordinated this work, and it was therefore extremely efficient.

Elsewhere in western Europe the medieval Inquisition continued to exist, but it proved totally ineffective when it came to dealing with the Protestant Reformation of the early sixteenth century. When initial attemps at securing a reconciliation between

the Protestant movements and Rome had failed, Pope Paul III re-
organized the papal Inquisition, using the Spanish Inquisition as
his model. In 1542 he created in Rome the Congregation of the
Inquisition, which is better known as the Holy Office, which was
responsible to the pope for co-ordinating and directing the work of
provincial inquisitors, and which acted as a final court of appeal in
heresy cases. The reformed Roman Inquisition thus became an
integral part of Counter-Reformation Catholicism, but its history,
like that of the Spanish Inquisition, lies outside the scope of this
book.

Protestant Europe, while rejecting much that it found offensive
in the Catholic tradition, was almost unanimous in its acceptance
of the teachings of the late medieval Church about the necessity of
religious coercion. It was quite natural that Protestants should
have wished to persecute Catholics, because Catholics had no
hesitation in persecuting them, but no such defence can be offered
for some forms which Protestant persecution took. Calvin, for
example, caused Servetus to be denounced to the Inquisition of
Marseilles, because Servetus did not believe in the doctrine of
the Trinity, and when he evaded the inquisitors and came to Protestant Geneva, Calvin had him burnt alive for heresy. This was
not an isolated and a-typical case: as many witches were burnt
in Protestant countries, including New England, as perished at
the hands of the Roman Inquisition in the post-Reformation
period.

The sad truth would seem to be that truly tolerant societies are
very rare, and that the desire to persecute individuals or groups
who flout the received orthodoxy, whatever it may be, is a deeply-
rooted human instinct. Such behaviour certainly antedated the
Inquisition, which was set up in order to moderate popular zeal
against heretics. The Church's reasons for resorting to coercion
are comprehensible, in that its leaders were the products of the
society in which they lived and therefore thought of the persecution of heretics as normal.

But society is not static, and by adopting the religious attitudes
of a particular period as part of its official policy the Church lost
flexibility. Pope Gregory IX and his successors, when establishing
the Inquisition, were endorsing attitudes prevalent in the West in
the eleventh and twelfth centuries, when membership of a single
Church had been regarded as axiomatic, and when heretics had
been spontaneously persecuted by the population at large. That
society had been very conservative in character, but it changed
considerably in the later medieval centuries and became more
diversified, whereas the Church sought, through the Inquisition,
to preserve a kind of religious conformity which had belonged to an

earlier age. Of its nature such a policy could not be successful, and consequently the Church came to have much less power at the end of the Middle Ages than it had had in the earlier centuries before it had introduced coercive measures.

Further reading

General histories of the Inquisition

H.C. Lea, *A History of the Inquisition in the Middle Ages* (3 vols., New York, 1888; reprinted 1955) remains the only definitive work on the subject.

E. Vacandard, *The Inquisition: a Critical and Historical Study of the Coercive Power of the Church* (English trans. B.L.Conway, London, 1908) remains valuable because it sets the Inquisition in its full historical context.

G.G. Coulton, *The Inquisition* (New York, 1929).
The Death Penalty for Heresy from 1184 to 1921, in the series *Medieval Studies* XVIII (London, 1924). The early sections are useful.

J. Guiraud, *L'Inquisition mediévale* (Paris 1928; reprinted 1978; English trans. E.C.Messenger, *The Mediaeval Inquisition*, London, 1929).

A.S. Turberville, *Mediaeval Heresy and the Inquisition* (London, 1920) has the merit of brevity although the early chapters on heresy should be used with caution.

General histories of heresy

M.D. Lambert, *Medieval Heresy. Popular Movements from Bogomil to Hus* (London, 1977) is the most comprehensive and up-to-date study.

G. Leff, *Heresy in the Later Middle Ages. The Relation of Heterodoxy to Dissent, c. 1250—c.1450* (2 vols., Manchester, 1967).

H. Grundmann, *Ketzergeschichte des Mittelalters* (Göttingen, 1963).

J.J.I. von Döllinger, *Beiträge zur Sektengeschichte des Mittelalters* (2 vols., Munich, 1890; reprinted 1960) is a collection of Latin sources about heresy throughout this period.

Chapter 1

R.W. Southern, *Western Society and the Church in the Middle Ages*, in the *Pelican History of the Church* series, II (London,

1970), is essential reading for anybody who wishes to understand the medieval Church.

J. Leclercq, F. Vandenbroucke, and L. Bouyer, *The Spirituality of the Middle Ages*, trans. by the Benedictines of Holme Eden Abbey, Carlisle, in the series *History of Christian Spirituality*, II (London, 1968).

N. Cohn, *The Pursuit of the Millennium* (London, 1957), a stimulating account of medieval millennarian movements which goes beyond the chronological limits of this work.

E. Le Roy Ladurie, *Montaillou. Cathars and Catholics in a French Village, 1294–1324* (English trans. by B.Bray, London, 1978), a detailed account of the life and beliefs of a medieval peasant community.

A. Murray, 'Piety and Impiety in Thirteenth-Century Italy', *Studies in Church History* VIII (1971), deals chiefly with the religious attitudes of urban society.

J. Le Goff, ed., *Hérésies et sociétés dans l'Europe préindustrielle, 11e–18e siècles* (Paris, 1968) contains much valuable information about religious convictions in the later Middle Ages.

Chapter 3

R.I. Moore, *The Origins of European Dissent* (London, 1977), an excellent account of heresy in the West, up to and including Catharism.

S. Runciman, *The Medieval Manichee. A Study of the Christian Dualist Heresy* (Cambridge, 1947) traces the origins of Catharism, although more recent work has led some scholars to question the chain of descent from Manicheism which is argued in this work.

A. Borst, *Die Katharer*, in the series *Schriften der Monumenta Germaniae Historica* XII (Stuttgart, 1953).

J. Guiraud, *Cartulaire de Notre Dame de Prouille, précédé d'une étude sur l'albigéisme languedocien au XIIe et XIIIe siècles* (2 vols., Paris, 1907). Despite its age, the long introduction in volume one is the best available statement of Cathar beliefs.

C. Thouzellier, *Catharisme et Valdéisme en Languedoc à la fin du XIIe et au début de XIIIe siècle. Politique pontificale — controverses. Série 'Recherches'* XXVII, Publications de la Faculté des Lettres et Sciences humaines de Paris (Paris, 1966). This is the best modern account of the origins of the Waldensians.

W.L. Wakefield and A.P. Evans, eds. and trans., *Heresies of the High Middle Ages*, in the series *Records of Civilization. Sources and Studies* LXXXI (New York, 1969), an excellent translation of the chief texts relating to heresy in this period, with commentary.

J. Sumption, *The Albigensian Crusade* (London, 1978) is a good military history of this war.

G. Koch, *Frauenfrage and Ketzertum im Mittelalter: Die Frauen-bewegung im Rahmen des Katharismus und des Walden-sertums und ihre sozialen Wurzeln (XII—XIV Jahrhundert)*, in the series *Forschungen zur mittelalterlichen Geschichte* IX (Berlin, 1962), deals with the rôle of women in heretical movements.

Chapter 3

H. Maisonneuve, *Études sur les origines de l'Inquisition*, in the series *L'Église et l'état au moyen âge* VII (2nd ed., Paris, 1960). A valuable study of legislation against heresy in civil and canon law.

P. Fournier, *Les officialités au moyen âge: étude sur l'organisa-tion, la compétence et la procédure des tribunaux ecclésias-tiques ordinaires en France, de 1180 à 1308* (Paris, 1880), a study of bishops' courts.

A. Luchaire, *Innocent III. Le Concile de Latran* (Paris, 1908), a straightforward account of the Fourth Lateran Council and what it achieved.

M.H. Vicaire, *Saint Dominic and his Times* (trans. K.Pond, London, 1964).

W.A. Hinnebusch, *A History of the Dominican Order: Origins and Growth to 1550* (New York, 1965).

J. Moorman, *A History of the Franciscan Order from its Origins to the Year 1517* (Oxford, 1968).

T.C. Van Cleve, *The Emperor Frederick II of Hohenstaufen* (Oxford, 1972).

Chapters 4 and 5

H.C. Lea, *The Inquisition of the Middle Ages. Its Organisation and Operation* (London, 1963) is, with an historical introduction by W.Ullmann, a reprint of the relevant chapters of Lea's main work.

G. Le Bras, *Les Institutions de la Chrétienté médiévale*, in the series *Histoire de l'Église* XII, contains a good brief account of the organization of the Inquisition.

Bernard Gui, *Manuel de l'Inquisiteur*, ed. and trans. into French by G.Mollat, 2 vols., in the series *Les Classiques de l'histoire de France au Moyen Age* VIII–IX (Paris, 1926), a text book on Inquisition procedure written by an inquisitor of Toulouse.

Nicholas Eymerich, *Le Manuel des Inquisiteurs*, trans. into French by L.Sala-Molins, École pratique des Hautes Éfudes, Sorbonne, VIe Section, Sources economiques et sociales, in the series *Le savoir historique* VIII (Paris, 1973). A text book written by a fourteenth-century Aragonese inquisitor.

J.T. McNeille and H.M. Gamer, *Medieval Handbooks of Penance: a translation of the principal 'Libri Poenitentiales' and Selections from Related Documents*, in the series *Records of Civilization* XXIX (New York, 1938), gives an account of ordinary penances awarded in the confessional.

Ullmann, W., 'The defence of the Accused in the Medieval Inquisition', *Irish Ecclesiastical Record* 73 (1950).

Chapter 6

W.L.Wakefield, *Heresy, Crusade and Inquisition in Southern France, 1100–1250* (London, 1974) contains a translation of William Pelhisson's chronicle.

C. Molinier, *L'Inquisition dans le Midi de la France au XIIIe et au XIVe siècle* (Paris, 1880).

G.W. Davis, *The Inquisition at Albi, 1229–1300* (New York, 1974).

Y. Dossat, *Les crises de l'Inquisition toulousaine au XIIIe siècle (1233–1273)* (Bordeaux, 1959).

R.W. Emery, *Heresy and Inquisition in Narbonne*, in the series *Studies in History, Economics and Public Law*, Faculty of Political Science of Columbia University, no. 480 (New York, 1941).

J.M. Vidal, 'Les derniers ministres de l'albigéisme en Languedoc: leurs doctrines', *Revue des Questions historiques* 79 (1906), gives a good account of Pierre Autier.

C. Douais, ed., *Documents pour servir à l'histoire de l'Inquisition dans le Languedoc* (2 vols., Paris, 1900; reprinted, Paris, 1977), a useful selection of Inquisition documents in Latin.

Cahiers de Fanjeaux have appeared annually since 1966 under the patronage of the Faculté des Lettres et des Sciences humaines of the University of Toulouse and the Institut catholique de Toulouse, and are concerned with the religious history of Languedoc in the thirteenth century.

Chapter 7

C.H. Haskins, 'Robert le Bougre and the Beginnings of the Inquisition in Northern France', in Haskins, *Studies in Mediaeval Culture* (New York, 1929), deals with the northern French Inquisition in the thirteenth century.

R. Kieckhefer, *Repression of Heresy in Medieval Germany* (Liverpool, 1979), a general survey, *inter alia*, of the work of the Inquisition in Germany. More specialized studies of the same subject:

L. Förg, *Die Ketzerverfolgung in Deutschland unter Gregor IX. Ihre Herkunf, ihre Bedeutung und ihre rechtlichen Grundlagen*, in the series *Historische Studien* CCXVIII (Berlin, 1932).

B. Kaltner, *Konrad von Marburg und die Inquisition in Deutschland* (Prague, 1882).

P.P. Bernard, 'Heresy in Fourteenth Century Austria', *Medievalia et Humanistica* X (1956).

There is no general survey of the work of the Inquisition in Italy, but see:

M. d'Alatri, *L'Inquisizione francescana nell'Italia centrale nel secolo XIII* (Rome, 1954).

J.V.A. Fine, *The Bosnian Church. A New Interpretation*, in the series *East European Monographs* X (New York, 1975), a study of Bosnian Catharism.

Chapter 8

M. Barber, *The Trial of the Templars* (Cambridge, 1978).

G. Lizerand, ed. and trans., *Le dossier de l'affaire des Templiers* (Paris, 1923; reprinted 1964), the sources for the trial.

D.L. Douie, *The Nature and the Effect of the Heresy of the Fraticelli*, in the University of Manchester Historical Series LXI (Manchester, 1932).

M.D. Lambert, *Franciscan Poverty* (London, 1961) deals with the wider aspects of the Spiritual movement in the Franciscan order.

M. Reeves, *The Influence of Prophecy in the Later Middle Ages* (Oxford, 1969), on the effects of Joachim of Fiore's teaching.

R.E. Lerner, *The Heresy of the Free Spirit in the Later Middle Ages* (Berkeley, 1972).

E.W. McDonnell, *The Beguines and Beghards in Medieval Culture, with special emphasis on the Belgian Scene* (New Brunswick, 1954), useful material on the character and function of these communities.

S. Wessley, 'The thirteenth-century Guiglielmites: salvation through women' in D. Baker, ed., *Medieval Women, Studies in Church History, Subsidia* I (Oxford, 1978), on the cult of Guiglielma at Milan.

Chapter 9

There are innumerable books on Joan of Arc. The documents of the case are published by:

P. Champion, ed., *Procès de condamnation de Jeanne d'Arc* (2 vols., Paris, 1920—1).

R. Pernoud, *The Retrial of Joan of Arc. The Evidence at the Trial for her Rehabilitation, 1450—6* (New York, 1955).

The same is true of Gilles de Rais. The documents of his trial are published in modern French by:

G. Bataille, *Le procès de Gilles de Rais* (Montreuil, 1965). Witchcraft in general has a voluminous literature, but the following works are recommended for the fifteenth century:

R. Kieckhefer, *European Witch Trials. Their Foundations in Popular and Learned Culture, 1300—1500* (London, 1976).

J.B. Russell, *Witchcraft in the Middle Ages* (Ithaca, 1972).

A.C. Kors and E. Peters, eds., *Witchcraft in Europe, 1100—1700. A Documentary History* (London, 1973) gives some of the key sources in English translation with commentary.

M. Spinka, *John Hus: a Biography* (Princeton, 1968).

H. Kaminsky, *A History of the Hussite Revolution* (Berkeley, 1967) can only be used by people with some background knowledge of the subject.

H. Kamen, *The Spanish Inquisition* (London, 1965) is a good modern treatment of this theme.

The Rise of Toleration (London, 1967) gives a good brief survey of Catholic and Protestant religious coercion in the post-Reformation period.

Index